everyday cooking
WITH THE
HALOGEN OVEN

everyday cooking
WITH THE
HALOGEN OVEN

Paul Brodel and Carol Beckerman

SELLERS
PUBLISHING

A Quintet Book

Published by Sellers Publishing, Inc.
161 John Roberts Road, South Portland, Maine 04106
Visit our Web site: www.sellerspublishing.com
E-mail: rsp@rsvp.com

ISBN: 978-1-4162-0692-7
e-ISBN: 978-1-4162-0746-7
Library of Congress Control Number: 2011935638
QTT.HOCB

This book was conceived, designed, and produced by
Quintet Publishing Limited
6 Blundell Street
London N7 9BH
United Kingdom

Food Stylist: Maud Eden
Photographer: Ria Osborne
Art Director: Michael Charles
Designer: Melissa Alaverdy
Project Editor: Alison Hissey
Editorial Director: Donna Gregory
Publisher: Mark Searle

Quintet Publishing would like to thank Andrew James, Flavorwave, Morningware Inc., Coopers of
Stortford and JML for the supply of halogen ovens.

10 9 8 7 6 5 4 3 2 1

Printed in China by 1010 Printing International Ltd.

CONTENTS

Introduction

A halogen oven does almost everything in one pot that it normally takes a conventional oven, stove, and barbecue grill to manage. It can bake, broil, roast, sauté, steam, fry, and grill—and it will do it better. All you have to do is plug it into a normal household electrical socket, and you are good to go!

A halogen oven is a fan oven, which combines the speed of a conventional oven with the instant heat of a halogen bulb to cook food more efficiently. It is basically a large glass bowl on a stand with a lid. The lid has a fan and an intense heat source—a halogen-heated lamp. It is small enough to sit on your countertop and large enough to feed a family of four comfortably. A very versatile piece of equipment, a halogen oven cooks slightly quicker and certainly more economically than conventional methods.

A halogen oven costs only a fraction of the sum of a conventional oven. As fuel costs rise, preheating a large conventional oven, even just to broil or bake for 30 minutes, becomes more expensive. A halogen oven almost never needs to be preheated. The amount of electricity needed to cook dinner is greatly reduced, so you save money in the long term.

Your halogen oven is also a much healthier cooking option. Overall you need far less fat to cook in a halogen oven than in a conventional oven or a skillet on the stovetop. But food isn't dry—moisture is locked in, while the fat tends to melt away, resulting in healthy and delicious meals.

Halogen ovens really excel with roasting and grilling. Chicken roasted in a conventional oven will often dry out, but cooked in your halogen oven, it will be moist and full of flavor. Red meat will be cooked to perfection, and fish is wonderful cooked in the halogen oven, as the flesh holds together beautifully and is moist and flavorful. The halogen oven is also great for quick dishes such as toasted sandwiches, especially those including cheese, so no need for expensive toasted sandwich makers any more.

Many vegetables are successfully cooked in the halogen oven, though some cook better than others. Porous Mediterranean vegetables such as zucchini and eggplant bake beautifully, staying tender with a chargrilled edge, while dense root vegetables such as carrots and rutabaga are best boiled on the stovetop, unless you cut them into julienne strips. Though potatoes are a root vegetable, they seem to be the exception, and, cooked in the halogen oven, you will get rave reviews for them every time. Whether roasted, baked, or cooked as French fries, they will be browned and crispy on the outside and soft and fluffy on the inside.

The whole family, but children especially, will enjoy the fast food aspect of halogen cooking, as burgers and bacon cook really quickly. You will find that a bacon sandwich in the morning for breakfast is not nearly so time-consuming with your halogen oven. Another way to save time and effort with a halogen oven is to grill your meat or fish on the top rack while baking or steaming your vegetables on the lower rack, and you can even cook meals all in one dish.

The halogen oven is incredibly versatile, and you will be amazed at the baked treats it can produce. Sweet creations such as luscious chocolate desserts will be meltingly soft and exquisite, and cinnamon rolls will be airy, delicate, and fluffy. Just swap the baking pans that you would normally use for large cakes for individual pans, which are more appropriate for the cooking style of the halogen oven. With just a few adjustments, you will discover alternative methods for cooking all your favorite recipes in the halogen oven.

Whether you use your halogen oven in conjunction with your conventional oven, or do all your cooking in it, it will prove itself invaluable in creating diverse and delicious meals to wow your friends and family. The halogen oven is officially no longer a fad, or a temporary blip on the kitchen horizon, it is here to stay, and the recipes in this book will inspire you to get the most out of it for every meal.

Buying a Halogen Oven

The most important thing to do when buying a halogen oven is to look at all the models available, and uncover as much information as you can. First, decide how you will use your halogen oven. Will it completely replace a regular oven, or will you use it along with the rest of your kitchen equipment?

Second, consider how many people you will be cooking for. Depending on the size of your oven, you can cook a complete meal for two or three, or parts of a meal, such as the meat or potatoes, for four to six people. As halogen ovens come in different sizes, decide which is the right size for your needs. If you are cooking for just one, you may think the very smallest is best. But look at the capacity of the oven. If you want to cook a whole chicken, it may be a good idea to buy a larger size, as it is better to have one slightly too big than too small. Consider also that the larger the oven, the bigger will be the pans you can fit into it, so it will be more versatile.

THINGS TO CONSIDER

- Will you use your halogen oven alone or alongside a regular oven?

- How many people do you usually cook for?

- What types of foods do you usually cook?

- What extra accessories will you need?

Third, because you need to plug the halogen oven into a nearby electric outlet, decide where the best location in the kitchen would be. The cable connects to the lid, which is where the motor is. That means when you lift the handle, the oven will automatically switch off, and you can remove the lid to either place it on a heatproof mat, or straight onto a specially designed lid stand (which can be purchased either with the oven or as an optional extra). The cable will still be plugged in, so you need enough space nearby to put the lid down. Some ovens have a lid that is hinged onto the glass bowl. If yours is one of these, you will need to make sure you have room above the oven to raise the lid, without it hitting anything above.

Finally, consider whether you want to select an oven that has extra accessories included in the price or whether you would prefer to purchase them separately, as needed. The extras available are an extender ring, which raises the height of the lid and enables you to cook a larger bird; a diffuser, which is a perforated tray sometimes used for steaming or covering a dish to prevent it burning; toast racks; and a lid stand.

Equipment

To fit your halogen oven to your needs, a range of extra accessories can be bought that have been specially designed for halogen oven cooking. These will ensure that your oven is perfectly suited to the types of foods you like to prepare.

Most halogen ovens come complete with an oven tray, and two racks, one high and one low. These are loose and just placed in the bottom of the glass bowl. The low one has short legs, which sit it close to the bottom, leaving a bigger gap between the rack and the lamp. The high one has longer legs, which puts it closer to the lamp. As a general rule, if the food is dense, use the low rack and cook for a longer time on a higher heat, and if the food is porous or very thin, cook on the high rack on a lower heat for a shorter period of time.

You will also need oven gloves and long tongs to move food around inside the oven and turn it over while it is cooking.

You will need a baking dish that will fit comfortably inside the oven, so there is room for the fan to move hot air around the dish in order to cook the food inside. Over time you will build up a collection of baking pans that are the ideal size for your own particular halogen oven.

You will find ordinary ramekin dishes invaluable for a great number of different recipes. You can use them for individual soufflés or desserts. You can put paper or silicone cups for muffins inside them, and even cook individual cinnamon or bread rolls. If using paper or silicone bakeware, make sure to place it only on the lower rack to prevent burning, and check regularly.

Foil can be used to make little parcels for cooking food. This is especially useful for cooking fish, because it will minimize cooking smells. You can also lay foil on the rack and place food directly on it, which makes cleanup faster.

Halogen Cooking Techniques

As with anything new, cooking in the halogen oven takes a little practice to perfect. The following is a guide to essential techniques that will help you to get the best results from your oven.

Temperatures and Timings

The symbols to the right of each recipe title give an indication of how long the recipe will take to prepare and cook. Times are in minutes unless otherwise stated.

 5   Preparation time: 5 minutes

  10   Cooking time: 10 minutes

While temperatures and timings specified in recipes are as accurate as possible, ovens from different manufacturers can vary significantly. In order to determine whether your oven cooks more or less quickly than average, before using your oven you should carry out the "Tortilla Test."

Even when you know your oven well, it is a good idea to check on your food as it cooks. If you find that food is burning on the surface, either lower the temperature or move the food to the lower rack if it is on the high one. You can also cover the food with foil. You can pierce the foil to let steam out, if you wish. Using foil will lengthen the cooking time slightly.

Most food will cook best when turned over a few times during the cooking process, but in a halogen oven you will not need to keep basting it with oil. In particular, if you want to cook a larger piece of meat, such as a whole chicken, you must turn it over a few times to allow it to cook all over. Cakes and rolls will also benefit from being turned over during baking.

THE TORTILLA TEST

Follow the Spanish tortilla recipe (page 37), using the exact temperature settings listed in the instructions, and checking on the tortilla regularly as you cook it. It will be clear when it is cooked, as the egg will have set and become opaque. If the time needed to reach this stage is longer than listed in the recipe, you will need to increase the cooking times listed in this book accordingly. If less time is needed to reach this stage, decrease cooking times accordingly. So if your halogen oven cooks the tortilla 10% quicker than stated in the recipe, decrease cooking times by 10%, and vice versa.

The heat from the lamp will brown dishes very quickly, but placing a bowl of water in the base of the oven will help prevent this. You can also cover the item with foil or the diffuser, turn the heat down, or move the item from the high rack to the low rack, if necessary.

When the cooking time has finished, remove the food immediately to prevent buildup of moisture in the oven. If you need to keep food warm, turn the heat down to about 60°F for a short time.

Grilling

The halogen oven is ideal for grilling. As a general rule, use the high rack, but if you are cooking meats that spit, place them on the lower rack. This will prevent the fat spitting upward onto the heating lamp, which is delicate and could be damaged. Place foil in the base of the oven to catch the fat.

Roasting

To roast meat, brush it with a little canola oil and place in a roasting pan. You can also cook meat directly on one of the racks, which has the benefit of the fat melting away. Place the oven tray or foil underneath to catch the drips of fat. If you want to be completely sure that meat is cooked properly, check the temperature of the meat with a meat thermometer.

Steaming

There are two ways to steam food in the halogen oven. For foods that are quick to steam, place the food on the lower rack of the oven and place the round oven tray on the upper rack. Fill the round tray with boiling water. Turn the oven to 480°F; the light will vaporize the water and the fan will move it around.

Alternatively, place the food in an ovenproof casserole dish or make a foil package; add a couple of tablespoons of water, lemon juice, or good-quality stock; and cover.

Cooking Vegetables

Many vegetables are ideal for steaming. To roast raw vegetables, cut them into small cubes or slices, about 1/2–1 inch in size, brush with canola oil, and place them on the oven tray on the high rack. Thicker vegetable slices should be cooked on the lower rack. Root vegetables will take the longest.

Vegetables often take longer to cook than meat, so if you want the vegetables to be ready at the same time as other food, you will need to start cooking them first. This is especially true for root vegetables, and carrots in particular.

TURNING

Halogen Ovens are great for many reasons, but despite the name the cooking itself is closer to broiling than baking. This means you'll need to turn some food to ensure even cooking.

- Pay close attention to turning instructions in the recipe

- Always use tongs when handling hot food

- If buying a new halogen oven, make sure it is big enough to turn food easily—consider buying a medium or large size rather than a small oven

Approximate Cooking Times

The following cooking times listed here are intended as a guide only. Much depends on the thickness of the food being cooked, the size of your halogen oven, and whether there is anything else in the oven cooking at the same time.

	Baking
SINGLE LAYER CAKE	Low rack with extender ring, 35 to 45 minutes at 350°F.
CUPCAKES	Low rack with extender ring, 25 to 40 mins at 350°F.
FLATBREAD	Low rack 13 minutes on each side at 400°F.
BREAD ROLLS	Low rack 15 to 25 minutes (depending on size) at 420°F.

	Vegetables
HARD VEGETABLES	Low rack 30–40 minutes at 400°F.
SOFT VEGETABLES	Low rack 15–20 minutes at 400°F.
ROOT VEGETABLES	Par boil first, then 45 minutes at 400°F, high rack.
JACKET POTATO	Low rack 25–40 minutes at 225°F.
ROAST POTATOES	Par boil first, then 45 minutes at 400°F, high rack.
FRENCH FRIES	High rack 10 minutes at 400°F.

	Roasted Meats
CHICKEN Small (2–3 lbs.) Medium (3–4.5 lb)	Low rack 45 minutes at 420°F, then 45 minutes at 350°F. Turn every 10–15 minutes. Low rack 45 minutes at 420°F, then 55 minutes at 350°F. Turn every 10–15 minutes.
LAMB JOINT (3 lbs.)	Low rack 460°F for 20 minutes, turning after 10 minutes, then 60 minutes at 350°F, turning every 15 minutes. For a well-done joint, continue cooking for up to 30 minutes more.
PORK JOINT (2 lbs.)	Rub with salt prior to cooking. Low rack. 420°F for 60 minutes, turning every 15 minutes, then 350°F for 30 minutes.
BEEF JOINT (2 lbs.)	Low rack 460°F for 30 minutes, turning every 10 minutes, then 350°F for 10 minutes (rare/blue), 30 minutes (medium), or 50 minutes (well done).

	Grilled Meats
STEAK	High rack 475°F. Rare: 2–5 minutes each side; Medium: 5–7 minutes each side; Well-done: 7–10 minutes each side.
PORK CHOPS	High rack 6–8 minutes each side at 400°F.
BACON	High rack 4–6 minutes at 425°F.
SAUSAGES	Low rack 10–12 minutes at 275°F.
CHICKEN BREAST	High rack 12–15 minutes at 375°F.
FISH (fillet portion)	Low rack 10–12 minutes at 400°F.
FISH (whole)	High rack 6–12 minutes each side at 480°F.

Care and Cleaning

Read your manufacturer's instructions for your particular oven, and always allow the bowl to cool before you clean it, as cold water may crack the hot glass.

Some ovens have a self-cleaning or wash setting, but if yours does not, these are the directions: After letting the oven cool, remove any small bits of food and pour off any oil or fat left in the glass bowl. Put 2–4 inches of cold water in the bottom of the bowl, add a little dish soap, and set the temperature to 60°F. Turn the timer to 10 or 15 minutes. The bulb will heat the water inside, and the fan will swirl the water around the bowl. This should result in a sparkling clean bowl. Pour off the soapy water, rinse with cool water, and dry with a clean cloth. Do not use abrasive cleaners or scouring pads on the glass bowl. You may leave the oven racks and oven tray in the oven during the cleaning process, which will loosen any particularly grimy bits, before washing them in the sink as normal.

Safety Advice

Keep the halogen oven on a stable heatproof surface, away from the edge. Make sure there is a suitable electric socket nearby, so that the cord does not hang over the edge of the work surface or touch anything hot while in use. Do not plug any other appliances into the same socket while you are using the halogen oven, and do not move the oven while it is in use.

Only use the halogen oven inside, and never on the stovetop or in a conventional oven.

The lid is very heavy. Make sure you have space and a heatproof mat immediately next to the oven, so that you can lift the lid off the glass bowl and place it straight onto the mat. If you have a stand for the lid, make sure it is on a flat heatproof surface, not near the edge, and has plenty of space around it. If your oven's lid is hinged onto the glass bowl, be certain you can raise the lid without letting it hit anything above.

All the electrics are in the lid, so do not place the lid in water.

The bowl gets very hot during use, especially at the top near the lamp, so have tongs and oven gloves on hand to lift food from the oven.

Do not use plastic in the oven. Only use ovenproof pans, baking dishes, foil, or the oven tray made for halogen ovens. Use silicone or paper muffin cases with caution.

Do not turn the timer backward, as this will damage it. If the timer is still running, and you need to turn off the oven, simply lift the handle, which works as an on/off switch. You should always use the handle to lift the lid on and off the glass bowl.

Always make sure the lid is securely attached to the glass bowl before switching on the oven.

If any faults develop, contact the retailer or the manufacturer.

BREAKFAST

Almond French Toast with Crispy Bacon

French toast always makes a great breakfast. In this recipe, the flavor of almonds blends beautifully with maple syrup and bacon, making a delicious combination.

8 strips bacon
1 1/2 cups sliced almonds
2 large eggs
1/3 cup whole milk
2 tbsp. maple syrup, plus extra for serving
1 tbsp. dark rum or Grand Marnier (optional)
4 (1/2-inch-thick) slices from a large brioche or challah loaf (or use 8 smaller slices)
3 tbsp. unsalted butter
confectioners' sugar, to serve

Serves 4

Lay the strips of bacon on the oven tray and cook in the halogen oven on the high rack at 375°F for about 3 minutes each side, until crispy. Remove from the tray and keep warm while you make the French toast. Wipe any remaining bacon grease off the oven tray.

Spread the sliced almonds in a thin layer on a large plate. In a large shallow bowl, whisk the eggs and milk together. Add the maple syrup and rum (if using) and whisk again. Soak 1 slice of bread in the egg mixture and press lightly on top of the almonds. Turn over and press the other side into the almonds. Repeat with the other 3 slices. Melt half the butter on the oven tray on the high rack at 350°F for 1–2 minutes, until foaming. Place two of the bread slices on the oven tray at a time, and cook on the high rack for 1 minute, turn the slices over, and cook for 3 minutes. Carefully turn again, and cook for another 2 minutes, or until golden brown and the nuts are slightly crispy at the edges. Watch carefully to make sure the almonds do not burn. Keep warm while you cook the other two slices, adding the extra butter as necessary.

Serve 1 slice of French toast per person, sprinkled with a little confectioners' sugar, and with 2 strips bacon.

ANOTHER WAY

Substitute white soda bread or raisin bread, and serve with whipped cream and fresh mixed berries instead of bacon and maple syrup. You could also substitute pecans or other nuts for the almonds, or dispense with them altogether.

Overnight French Toast with Caramelized Apples   +8h

This is such a great dish for holidays. When you have a houseful of guests, prepare it the night before, and amaze everyone with a delicious breakfast, seemingly effortlessly.

1/4 cup butter, softened
1/2 cup brown sugar
2 medium-size tart apples,
    peeled, cored, and sliced
3 eggs
3/4 cup milk
1 tsp. vanilla extract
6–7 slices French bread, cut on
    the diagonal
1 tbsp. sugar
1 1/2 tsp. ground cinnamon
1/2 tsp. ground nutmeg
confectioners' sugar and maple
    syrup, to serve

Serves 4–5

Make the caramelized apples. In a large skillet, melt the butter over medium heat, add the sugar, and cook for a minute. Add the apples, turn them over to coat with butter and sugar, and continue to cook over medium heat until the apples are tender and the sugar is slightly caramelized, about 5 minutes. Transfer to a 9-inch shallow baking dish, and set aside to cool completely.

In a large bowl, whisk together the eggs, milk, and vanilla extract. When the apples have cooled completely, dip the slices of bread in the egg mixture and place them on top of the apples in a single layer. Spoon the rest of the egg mixture over the bread.

In a small bowl, mix together the sugar, cinnamon, and nutmeg, and sprinkle half on top of the bread. Cover and chill for 8–24 hours.

To cook, remove the cover and set the dish on the low rack of the halogen oven. Cook for 15 minutes at 325°F. Turn the slices over, sprinkle the remainder of the spiced sugar over the top, and cook for 10 minutes more. Remove from the oven, place each portion on a plate, and serve sprinkled with confectioners' sugar on top and maple syrup on the side.

ANOTHER WAY

To make the recipe extra rich and creamy, substitute 3 tbsp. heavy cream for 3 tbsp. milk.

To make Peach–Pecan French Toast, replace the apples with sliced peaches and add 1/2 cup chopped pecans.

Welsh Cakes

These little spiced currant cookies are normally cooked on a griddle; in the halogen oven they do not take long to bake, so watch them carefully.

2 cups flour
1 tsp. baking powder
1 tsp. pumpkin pie spice
a pinch of salt
1/2 cup (1 stick) butter or
   margarine
1/2 cup plus 2 tbsp. superfine
   sugar
2/3 cup currants
1 egg, lightly beaten
1–2 tbsp. milk, as needed

Makes 20–25

In a large bowl, sift the flour, baking powder, pumpkin pie spice, and salt. Cut in the butter, either with a pastry cutter or with your fingers, until the mixture resembles fine breadcrumbs. Add the sugar and the currants, and mix until combined. Add the egg and mix to a soft dough, adding a little milk, if needed. Roll out to 1/4-inch thickness and cut into rounds with a 2 1/2-inch plain cutter. Place on the oven tray, and bake in batches on the high rack of the halogen oven at

ANOTHER WAY

Try making the Welsh cakes thicker, then, when cooled, split, and spread with butter and fruit conserve for a more filling treat.

425°F, for just 2–3 minutes each side. Transfer to a wire rack to cool completely. Serve, or store in an airtight container.

Breakfast Bars   +25

If you do not have time in the morning for a proper breakfast, grab a halogen-oven-baked breakfast bar and eat on the go! These are delicious and wholesome at the same time.

1/2 cup (1 stick) butter
2 tbsp. honey
1 cup brown sugar
2 1/2 cups rolled oats
1/4 cup golden raisins
1/4 cup chopped macadamia
   nuts
a pinch of salt

Makes 12 bars

In a medium saucepan, melt the butter and honey, add the sugar, and cook for 3 minutes over a gentle heat, until the sugar has dissolved. Add the oats, raisins, macadamia nuts, and salt, and stir well to combine. Transfer to the baking pan, and cook in the halogen oven on the low rack at 325°F for 10 minutes. Turn the heat down to 275°F, and cook for a further 30 minutes, until a lovely golden brown. Remove from the oven. Let cool in the pan for 5 minutes before cutting into 12 bars. Cool in the pan for another 10 minutes, then transfer the bars to a wire rack to cool completely. Store in an airtight container.

ANOTHER WAY

Melt 7 oz. semisweet chocolate in a bowl over hot water, add 1 tbsp. sunflower oil, and stir gently. Spread over the breakfast bars. Let cool before cutting and serving.

Almond Biscotti

These little cookie slices show just how versatile your halogen oven can be. Double-baked until crisp, they are just perfect to be dunked in coffee, as they soften beautifully without falling apart.

1 1/4 cups flour
1 tsp. baking powder
1/4 tsp. salt
1 egg
1/2 cup sugar
1/4 cup sunflower oil
1 tsp. almond extract
2/3 cup finely chopped
   blanched almonds

Makes 18–20

In a large bowl, sift together the flour, baking powder, and salt. In the bowl of a freestanding tabletop mixer, beat the egg and sugar together until light and fluffy. Add the sunflower oil and almond extract, and beat until combined and the mixture is thick and smooth. Reduce the speed and add the flour mixture. Finally, fold in the chopped almonds.

Turn the dough onto a floured work surface, flour your hands, and divide the dough in half. Transfer one half to a plate, cover, and keep cool. Transfer the other half to the oven tray, and mold it into a smooth log, 7 inches long, 2 1/2 inches wide, and 3/4 inch high. Place on the high rack of the halogen oven and bake at 325°F for 10 minutes, turn it over, and bake for another 10 minutes, or until light brown and slightly puffed. Remove from the oven and carefully cut the log on a slight diagonal into 3/4-inch-wide slices. Return to the oven's low rack, and bake for 4 minutes. Turn them over and bake for another 4 minutes, or until the cut surfaces of the biscotti have browned slightly and are dry to the touch. Transfer to a wire rack to cool completely, while you repeat the process with the other half of the dough. These can be stored for several days in an airtight container.

ANOTHER WAY

Add 1/4 cup chopped dried cranberries to the dough before baking, and dip the end of the biscotti in melted semisweet or white chocolate for an extra-special treat.

Blanched almonds are almonds with their skins removed. It is great fun and very satisfying to blanch them yourself. Just put them in a medium bowl and cover with boiling water. Leave for 2 minutes only, drain, and slide and pop the skins off. They should slide off the nuts easily.

Glazed Cinnamon Rolls

The subtle tangy flavor of sour cream and lemon in the pastry dough contrasts beautifully with the sweetness in the glaze. These rolls are a little tricky to bake in the halogen oven because you have to flip them over, but they are actually much better, because they stay so soft and light.

1/2 cup warm milk (110°F)

4 tbsp. plus 1 tsp. sugar, divided

1 envelope dry yeast

2 1/4 cups bread flour

1/2 tsp. salt

1/2 tsp. baking soda

1 small egg

1 tsp. vanilla extract

zest of 1 lemon

2 tbsp. sour cream

1/2 tsp. vegetable oil, for greasing

2 tbsp. butter, plus extra for greasing and brushing

1/4 cup dark brown sugar

1 tsp. ground cinnamon

Soft Icing

1 cup confectioners' sugar, sifted

2–3 tbsp. milk

1/2 tsp. glycerine (optional; it keeps the icing soft)

Makes 9

Grease an 8-inch square cake pan with a little butter.

Dissolve 1 tsp. sugar in the warm milk and sprinkle the yeast on top. Set aside for 10–15 minutes until frothy. In a large bowl, mix together the flour, salt, baking soda, and 4 tbsp. sugar. In a small bowl, whisk the egg, vanilla, lemon zest, and sour cream together. Make a well in the center of the flour and pour in the egg and sour cream mixture and the yeast liquid. Work to a soft dough, adding a little more milk if the dough feels too dry, or a little more flour if it feels too sticky. Turn dough out onto a lightly floured surface, and knead until you have a soft, smooth, and elastic dough. Alternatively, knead the dough in a freestanding tabletop mixer for 5 minutes.

Place dough in a bowl greased with 1/2 tsp. vegetable oil, turning it so that it is coated in oil all over, cover, and let rise in a warm place for about an hour, until it has doubled in size.

In a medium bowl, combine 2 tbsp. butter with the brown sugar and cinnamon. When the dough has doubled, turn out onto a lightly floured surface, knock back, knead lightly, and roll out to a 12 x 6-inch rectangle. Spread the butter and sugar mixture evenly over the surface, leaving a small margin around the edges. Roll tightly into a cylinder, sealing the far edge well. Turn the cylinder so that the seam is underneath, and cut

ANOTHER WAY

If your halogen oven is too small to fit an 8-inch square pan, put the rolls in greased ramekins and bake in batches, but still turn them over halfway through cooking.

into 9 equal-sized slices about 1 1/4 inches thick. Arrange the slices, touching, in the greased cake pan, cover, and let rise in a warm place for about 30 minutes. Brush the buns with a little melted butter, place the pan on the low rack in the halogen oven, and bake at 300°F for 10 minutes. Turn the buns out upside down onto a cookie sheet, then in one quick motion, slide them back into the pan, brush with a little more melted butter, and bake for another 10 minutes, or until golden brown. Let cool in the pan for 5 minutes, then transfer to a wire rack, placing them close together.

In a small bowl, beat the confectioners' sugar and just enough milk to make a smooth icing. Add the glycerine if using. Spread icing over the buns while they are still warm, allowing a little to run down the edges. Best served right away, while still warm.

Bacon Bagels

Homemade bagels are a real treat and much easier to make than you think. They are a dense bread, and, with the bacon for protein, will easily keep you going until lunch.

1 tsp. sugar
1 cup warm water (110°F)
1 envelope dry yeast
3 1/2 cups bread flour, plus extra
    for kneading
1 tsp. salt
vegetable oil, for greasing
16 strips bacon
salt and freshly ground black
    pepper
tomato ketchup, to serve

Makes 8

Dissolve the sugar in the warm water, add the yeast, and leave until frothy, about 10–15 minutes.

Sift 3 1/2 cups flour and 1 tsp. salt into the bowl of a freestanding tabletop mixer, make a well in the center, and add the yeast liquid. Using the dough hook of the mixer, knead for 5 minutes.

If the dough seems too sticky, add a little more flour; if it seems too dry, add a little more warm water. You need a firm but soft dough. Place in a greased bowl, turn the dough over to coat it all over, cover, and let rise for about an hour, or until doubled in size. Knock back and divide into 8 pieces. Roll each piece in your hands until it is perfectly round, then gently push your finger into the middle to make a hole, and twirl it around on your finger a little to widen the hole. Place on a cookie sheet, cover, and let rise for about an hour.

Fill a large pan with about 3–4 inches of water, and bring to a boil. Drop in the bagels, 2 or 3 at a time. They will rise to the surface almost immediately. Cook for 1 minute on each side, or 2 minutes if you prefer a chewier bagel. Using a

ANOTHER WAY

Before baking the bagels, brush them with beaten egg white and sprinkle with fennel or poppy seeds, then serve with cream cheese and smoked salmon, instead of bacon and ketchup.

slotted spoon, remove bagels from the water and place on the greased oven tray. Bake on the low rack of the halogen oven at 400°F for 6–7 minutes, flip them over with a spatula, and cook for 6–7 minutes more. When done, they should be a lovely golden brown color. Transfer to a wire rack to cool.

While the bagels are cooling, broil the bacon in batches on the oven tray in the halogen oven on the high rack at 400°F for 3–4 minutes per side, or until cooked and crispy. Drain on paper towels. To serve, split the bagels in half, add the bacon (2 strips per bagel), a little tomato ketchup, and season with salt and pepper. Serve immediately.

Carrot and Potato Hash Browns with Pancetta

This twist on the classic hash brown recipe is delicious with fried eggs and baked Boston beans.

1 large potato, peeled and grated
1 medium carrot, peeled and grated
1/2 medium onion, peeled and
   grated
1 medium egg
1 tbsp. flour
1/4 tsp. dried mixed Italian herbs
salt and freshly ground black pepper
1 tsp. olive oil, divided
1/4 cup diced pancetta

Serves 4

Dry the grated potato, carrot, and onion with paper towels. Place in a large bowl. Mix in the egg, flour, and dried herbs. Season with salt and pepper. Wipe the round oven tray with half the olive oil. Divide the potato–carrot mixture into fourths. Place them on the tray and form into round circles, pressing down on them to get out all the air. Drizzle with the remaining olive oil. Place the diced pancetta around the hash browns. Cook on the low rack of the halogen

ANOTHER WAY

Children love these tasty hash browns, and you could even add other vegetables to them to make a really healthy breakfast.

oven for 12 minutes at 450°F, then turn over the hash browns and place back in the oven for an additional 11 minutes.

Oven-Baked Rosti

A rosti is a bit like a small pancake but is made of coarsely grated potatoes and onions. Baking in the halogen oven is a really healthy way to make rostis. They are delicious as a breakfast dish with fried eggs and bacon.

2 cups coarsely grated peeled
   raw potatoes
1/2 cup coarsely grated raw onion
1 egg
1 tbsp. flour
salt and freshly ground black
   pepper
2 tbsp. canola or olive oil

Makes 4 rostis

Pat dry the potatoes and onion with some paper towels and place in a large mixing bowl. Mix in the egg and flour, then season with salt and pepper. Divide into 4 equal parts and shape into 4 burger-sized patties.

Pour half the oil onto the round oven tray and place the 4 patties on the tray. Place on the low rack in the halogen oven, drizzle with the rest of the oil, and cook at 500°F for 12 minutes. Turn the rostis over and cook for an additional 12 minutes until golden brown. Serve hot.

ANOTHER WAY

Rather than hand-grating the potatoes for the rosti, it is much quicker and easier to use a grater attachment on an electric mixer.

Meat-Lovers' Potato Skillet

Nothing grills as quickly as a halogen oven, which makes it ideal for preparing this recipe. The chorizo really helps to add flavor to the potato when cooking. Serve with fried eggs and grilled tomatoes.

1 large potato, peeled and diced
1/2 medium onion, sliced
2 chorizo sausages, sliced
2 strips bacon, chopped
1 tsp. olive oil
salt and freshly ground black
    pepper
1 slice thick-cut ham, sliced
    into strips

Serves 2

In a large bowl, mix the potato, onion, chorizo, bacon, and olive oil. Season with salt and pepper.

Tip mixture onto the round baking tray and set it on the low rack in the halogen oven. Cook at 450°F for 25 minutes, stirring every 7 minutes. Add the ham strips, stir, and cook for 2 minutes more. Remove and serve.

NOW TRY THIS...

THREE PEPPER BREAKFAST HASH

Follow the recipe as directed above, adding 1/2 red bell pepper, 1/2 yellow bell pepper, and 1/2 green bell pepper, diced, along with the chorizo and bacon.

SPICY SWEET POTATO SKILLET

Follow the recipe as above, substituting sweet potato for the white potato. Make the dice slightly larger than you would for white potato. Omit the bacon and ham, and instead add 1 small red chile, chopped and deseeded, and 1 small zucchini, chopped, along with the chorizo. Cook as directed above.

SMOKED SALMON SKILLET

Follow the recipe as above, omitting the onion, bacon, and chorizo, and instead adding in 1 green onion, finely chopped, along with the potato. Cook for 25 minutes, stirring every 7 minutes, then add 1 slice smoked salmon, chopped. Cook for 2 minutes more. Serve with scrambled eggs, with sour cream dip (page 114), if liked.

VEGETARIAN POTATO SKILLET

Follow the recipe as directed above, omitting the chorizo, bacon, and ham. Add in 1/2 red bell pepper, 1/2 medium zucchini, diced, 1 cup button mushrooms, and 1 tsp. Italian seasoning along with the potatoes and onions.

Sausage Patties

Store-bought sausage patties contain a lot of salt and fat. It is so much healthier to make them yourself, as you can control the ingredients. All you need to go with these patties is buttermilk biscuits and a few slices of ripe tomato.

1 1/2 lbs. premium low-fat
    ground pork
1/2 tsp. ground white pepper
1/2 tsp. ground ginger
1/2 tsp. ground sage
1 tsp. dried mixed Italian herbs
2 tsp. salt, or to taste
2/3 cup breadcrumbs
freshly ground black pepper
buttermilk biscuits and tomato
    slices, to serve

Serves 6

In a large bowl, using your hands, combine all the ingredients together, making sure that the herbs and spices are distributed evenly. Still using your hands, form the sausage meat into 6 patties, pressing the meat firmly together. You can use a hamburger press for this, if you have one. If you prefer small patties, make 12. Place them on the oven tray, sprinkle with some freshly ground black pepper, and cook on the high rack of the halogen oven at 400°F for 4–6 minutes. Turn them over, sprinkle with some more pepper, and cook for another 4–6 minutes, or until cooked through. Cook in batches if necessary. Serve immediately.

NOW TRY THIS...

TURKEY PATTIES

Mix 1 1/2 lbs. ground turkey, 1 small diced onion, 1 tbsp. chopped fresh parsley, 2 cloves garlic, 1/2 tsp. ground white pepper, 2 tsp. salt, 1/2 tsp. ground ginger, 1/2 tsp. red chile flakes, and 2/3 cup breadcrumbs. Mold the mixture into patties and cook as directed above.

APPLE AND MAPLE SAUSAGE PATTIES

Follow the sausage patties recipe as above, omitting the mixed Italian herbs and adding 1 medium apple, peeled, cored, and finely chopped, 2 tbsp. maple syrup, and 1/4 tsp. cinnamon when you mix together the ingredients. Cook as directed above. Serve with buttermilk biscuits and crispy bacon.

SAUSAGE PATTIES WITH ONION GRAVY

The patties are delicious with onion gravy for dinner. Follow the recipe as directed above to make the patties. To make the gravy, gently fry 2 sliced large onions in a little oil for 15 minutes. Add 1 tsp. flour and 1 tsp. Dijon mustard, and cook for 2 minutes. Gradually add 1 cup good-quality beef stock and 1 beef stock cube. Season and simmer until thickened. Serve with the patties and mashed potatoes.

Spanish Tortilla

This is a basic Spanish tortilla, but feel free to add some different ingredients, such as peas, chopped red bell pepper, ham, chorizo, fresh tomato, or cheese.

1 large potato, peeled and cut
    into small cubes
1/2 onion, sliced
1 tbsp. butter
1 tbsp. olive oil
4 medium eggs
1 tbsp. milk
1 tbsp. water
salt and freshly ground black
    pepper

Makes 4–6 slices

In a medium saucepan, boil the cubed potato for 6 minutes in boiling water, then drain and set aside.

Place a cup of boiling water into the base/glass bowl of the halogen oven. This helps to slow down the browning process.

Place the sliced onion on the round oven tray with the butter and oil.

Cook on the low rack in the halogen oven at 500°F for 6 minutes. Add the potatoes, mix well, and cook for 5 minutes more.

In a small bowl, mix the eggs with the milk, water, salt, and pepper. Pour the egg mixture over the potatoes. Lower the heat in the halogen oven to 300°F and cook for 12 minutes. Slice and serve hot or cold.

NOW TRY THIS...

HAM AND CHEESE

Follow the basic recipe, adding 1/4 cup chopped deli ham, 1/4 cup cheddar cheese, and 1/4 cup diced tomato to the egg mixture. Cook as directed above.

SPICY SAUSAGE

Follow the recipe as above, adding 1/4 cup chopped chorizo and 1/2 red bell pepper, diced, when you add the onions. Cook as directed above.

VEGETABLE FEAST

Follow the recipe as above, substituting 1/2 small red onion for the white onion. Add 1/2 red bell pepper, diced, 1/2 zucchini, diced, 4 mushrooms, sliced, 1/4 cup frozen peas along with the onions.

MEAT FEAST

Follow the recipe as above, adding 8 slices pepperoni, 1/4 cup cubed deli ham, and 1/4 cup cubed cooked chicken to the egg mixture. Cook as directed above. Serve with tomato sauce (page 59)

BROCCOLI AND STILTON

Follow the recipe as above, adding 1/4 cup crumbled stilton, and 1 cup parboiled broccoli torn into very small florets, to the egg mixture. Cook as directed above.

LUNCH

Turkey Pie

This is a great way to use up that leftover turkey from a roast. If you ever thought it was complicated to make a turkey pie, this recipe will prove you wrong!

Pastry
2 cups all-purpose flour
1/2 cup (1 stick) butter, cold (slice a bit to fit into processor)
1 tbsp. water
1 beaten egg, for glazing

Filling
1 medium onion, chopped
4 mushrooms, sliced
2 tsp. olive oil
1 tbsp. butter
salt and freshly ground black pepper
2/3 cup whole milk
1 tbsp. cornstarch
11 oz. cooked turkey (cubed)
2/3 cup heavy cream
1 chicken stock cube mixed with 4 tbsp. boiling water
1 tbsp. freshly chopped parsley

Serves 4

To make the pastry, place the flour, cold butter, and 1 tbsp. water into a food processor fitted with a mincing blade. Mix until the pastry forms a ball. Wrap the pastry in plastic wrap and chill in the refrigerator for 30 minutes.

To make the filling, put the chopped onion, mushrooms, olive oil, butter, and seasoning into a baking dish or deep pie pan. Place dish on the low rack in the halogen oven and cook at 500°F for 12 minutes, stirring twice during cooking.

Meanwhile, in a mixing bowl, mix a little of the milk with the cornstarch to dissolve it, then stir in the cubed turkey. Mix in the remaining milk and the cream, stock, and parsley. Pour the mixture into the dish, stir to combine with the onions and mushrooms, and cook for 10 minutes. Remove and stir.

Roll out the pastry to the size of the dish, place it on top of the filling, and brush with the beaten egg to glaze. Cook at 500°F for 12 minutes or until golden brown. Serve immediately.

ANOTHER WAY
Add 1 tbsp. chopped fresh tarragon to the filling for a very flavorful variation. You can also use this pastry as a topping for any number of different pie fillings.

Asian-Spiced Chicken Wings

This recipe will be a big hit and will bring you rave reviews. You could make extra sauce to serve with the wings, if you want.

3 lbs. chicken wings
2 cloves garlic, minced
1/2 tsp. salt
2 tbsp. soy sauce
2 tbsp. hoisin sauce
3 tbsp. honey
1 tsp. sesame oil
2 pinches cayenne pepper
freshly ground black pepper
1 green onion, green part only,
    finely chopped
1 1/2 tbsp. sesame seeds

Serves 4–8

With some kitchen shears, snip off the tips of the chicken wings and halve the wings at the joint. If desired, remove as much skin as you can.

In a large bowl, mix together the minced garlic, salt, soy sauce, hoisin sauce, honey, sesame oil, and cayenne pepper. Add the chicken wings to the bowl, and turn over to coat all over. Season with plenty of freshly ground black pepper. If you have time, place in the refrigerator to marinate for an hour or so. Transfer the chicken wings to the round oven tray, and cook on the high rack of the halogen oven at 450°F for 10 minutes, turning every 2–3 minutes. Turn the temperature down to 400°F and cook for 10–15 minutes more, or until cooked through, turning halfway through cooking time. Remove from the oven and stir in the green onion and sesame seeds. Serve immediately.

NOW TRY THIS...

THAI WINGS

Mix 1 tbsp. fish sauce with 1 cup coconut milk, zest and juice of 1 lime, 2 shredded kaffir lime leaves (optional), 1 bashed lemongrass stalk, 2 deseeded and sliced Thai chiles, and 2 sliced scallions. Marinade 3 lbs. chicken wings for an hour, then cook as for Asian-Spiced Chicken Wings.

CARIBBEAN WINGS

Mix 2 tbsp. red wine vinegar, 1 large grated onion, 2 tbsp. tomato paste, 4 crushed garlic cloves, 2 tsp. brown sugar, 1 very finely chopped habanero chile, and 2 tsp. anchovy paste. Marinade 3 lbs. chicken wings overnight, and cook as directed above.

HOT WINGS

Mix 1 tbsp. regular paprika with 1 tsp. each of salt, garlic salt, cayenne pepper, lemon pepper, white pepper, and ground cumin. Rub into 3 lbs. wings. Marinate for 15 minutes, and then cook as directed above. Melt 1 cup pepper sauce with 1 stick butter, 1 tsp. each garlic salt and cayenne pepper, and mix to combine. Pour over cooked wings and toss.

HERBY WINGS

Mix 1/2 cup olive oil with 2 tbsp. balsamic vinegar, 2 tbsp. fresh parsley, 1 tbsp. chopped fresh rosemary, 1/2 tbsp. chopped fresh lemon thyme, and salt and pepper. Marinate for 1 hour in the refrigerator and cook as directed above.

Chicken and Corn Enchiladas

Sautéed chicken and vegetables are wrapped up in tortillas before being baked in enchilada sauce, then topped with cheese. Make the dish as spicy as you like by varying the amount of chile in the sauce.

Enchilada Sauce

1 tbsp. canola oil
1 medium onion, finely chopped
2 cloves garlic, minced
1 tsp. chili powder, or to taste
1 (16-oz.) can chopped tomatoes
    in sauce
1 (5-oz.) can tomato paste
1 beef stock cube
2 tsp. sugar
1/4 cup freshly chopped cilantro
salt and freshly ground black pepper

Enchilada Filling

1 medium onion, finely chopped
1/2 cup eggplant in 1/2-inch cubes
1/2 cup zucchini in 1/2-inch cubes
1/2 red bell pepper in 1/2-inch cubes
8 cherry tomatoes
2 tbsp. canola oil, plus extra for greasing
3 boneless and skinless chicken breasts,
    cut into 1-inch pieces
1 tsp. chili powder
2 tsp. ground coriander
2 tsp. ground cumin
1/4 cup freshly chopped cilantro
1–2 tbsp. freshly chopped basil
1 red chile, seeded and finely chopped, or
    to taste
1 (8-oz.) can whole kernel corn, drained
1 (11-oz.) can baked beans in sauce

To Finish

1 tsp. olive oil
8 (6-inch) tortillas
2 cups shredded cheddar cheese
sour cream and chopped green onions,
    to serve

Makes 8

Make the enchilada sauce. In a large saucepan, heat the oil, add the onion, and cook for 5 minutes, until slightly softened. Add the garlic and cook over a gentle heat for 10 minutes. Add the chili powder and cook for 1 minute, stirring continuously. Add the tomatoes, tomato paste, stock cube, and sugar. Cover and simmer for 25 minutes. Add the cilantro and season with salt and pepper. Transfer to a bowl and set aside.

Make the filling. Place the vegetables on the oven tray, drizzle with a little canola oil, and place on the low rack of the halogen oven. Bake for 10 minutes at 400°F, turn the vegetables over, and cook for a further 5–10 minutes, or until they are slightly charred on the edges and tender. Remove from the oven and place in a large bowl.

In a large skillet, heat 1 tbsp. oil. When it is hot, but not smoking, add the chicken and sauté for 10 minutes, until browned and cooked through. Add the chili powder, coriander, and cumin, and cook for 1 minute, stirring continuously. Add

TIP

Sealing the tortillas by frying them in a little oil means they will not soak up too much of the sauce.

chicken to the charred vegetables, and mix in the cilantro, basil, red chile, corn, and baked beans.

Wipe the skillet, add 1 tsp. oil, and fry each tortilla for 1 minute per side, adding a little more oil as necessary. Lay the tortillas on the work surface. Spoon about 5–6 tbsp. of the chicken and vegetable filling into the middle of each tortilla. Roll up tightly and place side by side in a greased baking dish. Spoon enchilada sauce on top, and sprinkle with cheddar cheese. Cover and cook on the low rack at 350°F for 30 minutes, then remove the lid and cook for another 10 minutes, or until piping hot and nicely browned on top. Sprinkle with chopped green onions and serve with sour cream.

Chicken Fajitas with Pico de Gallo

These are delicious and authentic-tasting fajitas and the Pico de Gallo is a great accompaniment.

Pico de Gallo

8 ripe plum tomatoes, seeded and chopped
1 small red onion, finely chopped
2 cloves garlic, crushed
1 jalapeño pepper, halved and seeded
1 tbsp. olive oil
juice of 1 lime
5 tbsp. freshly chopped cilantro
salt and freshly ground black pepper

Marinade

1/4 cup honey
1/4 cup soy sauce
2 tsp. dried basil
2 tsp. dried oregano
1 tbsp. tomato ketchup
2 tbsp. brown sugar
2 tbsp. olive oil
2 tbsp. red wine vinegar
1 1/2 tsp. ground ginger
freshly ground black pepper
4 skinless and boneless chicken breasts
1/2 tsp. salt
1 tsp. chili powder

For the Fajitas

2 red bell peppers, finely sliced
2 green bell peppers, finely sliced
2 large onions, finely sliced
8–10 flour tortillas, warmed
sour cream, to serve

Serves 4

Put all the ingredients for the Pico de Gallo in a medium bowl, mix well, and chill for at least 8 hours.

Prepare the marinade. In a medium bowl, combine the honey, soy sauce, basil, oregano, ketchup, brown sugar, olive oil, red wine vinegar, ground ginger, and pepper. Place the uncooked chicken on a plate, and season with the salt and chili powder. Slice the chicken into strips, place it in the marinade, and turn it over to coat it all over. Chill for 1–10 hours. Remove chicken from the marinade, place the marinade in a small saucepan, and bring to a boil. Remove from the heat and transfer to a small bowl. Place the chicken on the oven tray on the high rack of the halogen oven, drizzle with a little marinade, and cook at 425°F for about 8 minutes, turning the chicken over occasionally, and basting with the marinade. When it is no longer pink in the middle, remove from the oven and keep warm. Place the peppers and onions in a shallow baking dish, and cook on the high rack for

ANOTHER WAY

Add guacamole to serve on the side. Mix 2 peeled, pitted, and chopped avocados with 2 tsp. lemon juice, 1 tsp. Worcestershire sauce, 2 cloves minced garlic, and 2 tsp. each of dried red pepper flakes and minced fresh onion.

about 8 minutes at 450°F, stirring occasionally, and basting with a little marinade. When the peppers and onions are tender, transfer the chicken to the baking dish, stir to combine with the pepper, and onion, and return to the halogen oven on the high rack. Cook for 5 minutes at 350°F, or until piping hot and slightly charred on the edges. Divide the chicken and peppers between the tortillas, and roll up. Serve with the Pico de Gallo, and the sour cream on the side.

Jerk Chicken with Mango Salsa

This Caribbean recipe is meant to be fiery, but you can reduce the amount of chile for a milder version. Don't omit it altogether though; this recipe brings out the chile flavor as well as the heat.

Jerk Seasoning
1 tbsp. ground allspice
4 cloves garlic, peeled and crushed
1 tbsp. canola oil
2 scotch bonnet chiles
1 tsp. black pepper
a pinch of salt
1 tsp. ground coriander seeds
1/2 tsp. ground cinnamon
1 tsp. ground ginger
2 tsp. chili powder
juice of 1 lime
1/2 tsp. garlic powder

Serves 4

Jerk Chicken
1 tbsp. mayonnaise
6 chicken thighs, boned and skinned

Mango Salsa
1 mango, peeled, pitted, and finely chopped
2 green onions, finely sliced
2 tomatoes, deseeded and diced
juice of 1 lime
1 tbsp. chopped fresh cilantro
1 jalapeño pepper, chopped

Place the jerk seasoning ingredients into a food processor and blend thoroughly. In a bowl, mix 1 tbsp. jerk seasoning and 1 tbsp. mayonnaise, then add the chicken thighs, coat, and allow to marinate for at least 10 minutes in the refrigerator (overnight is even better).

Cook in a round oven tray on the high rack of the halogen oven at 400°F for 7 minutes each side or until cooked, turning halfway though the cooking time.

For the mango salsa combine all the ingredients and serve with the jerk chicken.

TIP
The remaining jerk seasoning will keep in a sealed container in the refrigerator for up to two weeks.

Tuna Melt

This potato and tuna melt makes a fantastic, warming lunch on a chilly day. Nothing can be more comforting than seeing the cheese bubble under the intense halogen light.

4 medium baking potatoes
1 tsp. olive oil
1/4 tsp. salt
1 cup drained canned tuna
4 green onions, finely chopped
3 tbsp. mayonnaise
1 tbsp. tomato ketchup
1/4 tsp. paprika (smoked is good)
2 tbsp. freshly chopped parsley
1/2 cup shredded cheddar cheese or Swiss cheese

Serves 4

Wash and dry the potatoes, prick them with a fork, rub with the oil, and sprinkle with salt. Place them on the low rack of the halogen oven and cook at 450°F for 45–70 minutes, depending on the size of the potatoes or until cooked. Turn over every 15 minutes.

When cooked, slice potatoes in half lengthwise. Scoop out the pulp into a mixing bowl. Add the tuna, onions, mayonnaise, ketchup, paprika, and parsley. Mix well. Fill the potato skins with the

ANOTHER WAY
Potatoes baked in the halogen oven are delicious with any number of fillings. Try substituting cubed ham or canned salmon for the tuna.

mixture, and sprinkle with the grated cheese. Cook the potatoes on the high rack at 450°F for 5 minutes or until golden brown.

47

LUNCH

Steak Burgers with Mozzarella Cheese

A hamburger made with good-quality meat can be just as good as a steak. Mixing rump steak with a cheaper cut keeps the hamburger moist and the cost down.

9 oz. round steak
9 oz. chuck steak or beef shank
1 tbsp. olive oil, plus extra for greasing
1/2 small onion, finely chopped
1/4 cup finely grated Parmesan cheese
1/4 cup freshly chopped parsley
1 tsp. dried mixed Italian herbs
salt and freshly ground black pepper
1 small egg, lightly beaten
4 oz. mozzarella cheese

Makes 4

Cut the meat into cubes, trimming off any large pieces of fat. Chop or grind the meat and put into a large bowl.

In a small skillet, heat 1 tbsp. olive oil, add the onion, and sauté until softened, about 5 minutes. Add the onion to the beef, along with the Parmesan cheese, parsley, Italian herbs, salt, and pepper. Using your hands, bind the mixture together with the egg. Divide the mixture into 8 portions and shape them into patties with your hands. Place 4 patties on a work surface. Slice the mozzarella cheese into 4 parts, and place a slice on the 4 patties. Top with the remaining patties and seal the edges well to prevent the cheese from oozing out.

Grease the oven tray and place the hamburgers on it. Set the tray on the high rack of the halogen oven and cook at 425°F for 5–6 minutes. Turn the patties over and cook for another 5–6 minutes, or until lightly browned and cooked through. Serve immediately.

TIP

If you grind the meat yourself, handle it as little as possible, and you will be rewarded with a tender hamburger with a delicious flavor. Try to avoid chopping the meat in a food processor, as it is very easy to overwork the meat, which makes it tough.

Beef Cannelloni in Tomato Sauce

A rich Italian dish, cannelloni is pasta rolled around a delicious meat sauce, covered with tomato sauce, and baked in the oven.

vegetable oil, for greasing
1 lb. 2 oz. ground beef
1 large onion, finely chopped
2 cloves garlic, crushed
1 (16-oz.) can chopped tomatoes in sauce
2 (5-oz.) cans tomato paste
1/3 cup good-quality beef stock
1 beef stock cube
1 tsp. sugar
1 tsp. dried mixed Italian herbs
salt and freshly ground black pepper
8 dry lasagne noodles
2 tsp. cornstarch, mixed with a little water
2 cups tomato sauce (page 59)
finely grated Parmesan cheese, to serve

Serves 4

Grease a baking dish with a little vegetable oil. In a large saucepan, dry-fry the beef until browned, then drain off and discard the fat. Return the beef to the saucepan, add the onion and garlic, and cook for 10 minutes, until the onion has softened. Stir in the tomatoes, tomato paste, stock, stock cube, sugar, herbs, salt, and pepper. Cover, and simmer gently for 40 minutes. Add the cornstarch mixture to the meat sauce, stirring continuously. Simmer for 5 minutes, remove pan from the heat, and let cool for 10 minutes.

While the beef is simmering, bring a large saucepan of water to a boil, and cook the lasagne noodles for 10 minutes. Drain and refresh in cold water.

ANOTHER WAY

For a variation, add 1/2 cup ricotta cheese and 1 cup fresh spinach leaves to the meat sauce, and sprinkle with shredded cheddar cheese before baking.

Place 2 tbsp. meat sauce on each cooked lasagne noodle, and roll up tightly. Place them side by side in a baking dish. Ladle over the tomato sauce, cover with a lid or foil, and bake on the low rack of the halogen oven at 350°F for 35 minutes, or until piping hot. Sprinkle with a little Parmesan cheese before serving.

Philly Cheese Steak

The intense radiant heat of the halogen oven helps to cook and brown the meat very quickly, making this another fast and easy everyday recipe that is great for a tasty, filling lunch.

1 onion
1 green bell pepper
1 tbsp. oil
1/2 tsp. garlic salt
1/2 tsp. coarsely ground black pepper
6 oz. raw ribeye steak
4 slices provolone cheese
2 kaiser buns, halved

Serves 2

Thinly slice the onion and pepper, and place in a bowl. Add the oil, garlic salt, and pepper, and mix. Tip mixture onto the round oven tray and place in the halogen oven on the low rack. Cook at 500°F for 5 minutes.

Thinly slice the steak and add to the round tray, stir, and cook for a further 8 minutes at 500°F, stirring every 2–3 minutes.

ANOTHER WAY

For a delicious taste variation, stir in 2 tbsp. sweet chilli sauce in the last 2 minutes of cooking.

Put 2 slices cheese into each bun. Add the beef mixture and serve hot.

Quesadillas with Refried Beans

Cooked in the halogen oven, this traditional Mexican recipe will make a delicious treat for all the family in no time at all.

1/2 red onion, sliced
1/2 tbsp. olive oil
2 cups refried beans
4 flour tortillas
1 tomato, diced
1/2 red bell pepper, sliced
1 jalapeño pepper, sliced,
  seeds removed
1/2 cup diced cooked chicken
4 tbsp. shredded pepperjack
  cheese
salt and freshly ground black
  pepper

Serves 2

Place the red onion with the olive oil on the round oven tray on the low rack in the halogen oven. Cook at 500°F for 5 minutes. Pour in the refried beans, mix, and cook for 3 minutes or until thoroughly heated. Remove and pour into a bowl.

Place a flour tortilla on a clean round oven tray. Spread half of the refried beans on the tortilla. Top with half the diced tomatoes, half the peppers and jalapeño, half the chicken, and half the cheese. Place on the low rack and cook at 500°F for 6 minutes, then add another tortilla wrap on top to form a sandwich. Cook for

1 minute more. Remove from the oven and keep warm while cooking the other quesadilla.

Slice into quarters like pizza and serve with lettuce and sliced tomato.

NOW TRY THIS...

CUBAN SANDWICH QUESADILLA

Spread the bottom tortilla with a thin layer of yellow mustard, then add 1 slice deli ham, 1 slice roast pork, 1 thinly sliced dill pickle, and 1 slice Swiss cheese. Grill on the low rack at 500°F for 6 minutes, before adding another tortilla on top, and cooking for 1 minute more.
.

QUESADILLAS DE CARNE

Follow the recipe as above, substituting 1/4 cup cooked ground beef, seasoned with salt and black pepper, for the cooked chicken. Serve with shredded lettuce and slices of avocado and tomato.

CORN QUESADILLAS

Follow the recipe as above, omitting the refried beans, and instead spreading the tortillas with 2 tbsp. mayonnaise mixed with 1 tbsp. lime juice. Add 1 cup fresh corn kernels along with the diced tomato. Cook as directed above.

Mini Quiches 30 45

This is a very useful pastry for any type of quiche, and it's so simple to make it in a halogen oven.

Shortcrust Pastry
1 1/2 cups all-purpose flour
1/2 cup (1 stick) salted butter
a pinch of salt
1 tbsp. cold water

Quiche Filling
3 eggs
1/4 cup milk
2 tbsp. heavy cream
1 cup shredded cheddar
    cheese
3 strips bacon, chopped
1/4 medium onion, chopped
salt and freshly ground black
    pepper
1 tomato, sliced

Serves 3

To make the shortcrust pastry, put the flour, butter, and salt into a food processor. Process until the mixture has the consistency of fine breadcrumbs, then mix in the cold water until a dough is formed. Wrap the dough in plastic wrap and chill for 20 minutes, then remove it from the fridge and divide it into 3 balls. On a lightly floured surface, roll out each ball into a circle.

Lightly grease 3 ramekin dishes, then line each one with a circle of pastry. With a fork, prick the pastry in the bottom of the dishes a couple of times. Then place a sheet of waxed paper, topped with baking beans (for baking blind), in each ramekin. Place the ramekins on the low rack of the halogen oven and cook at 400°F for 20 minutes.

Meanwhile, beat the eggs in a bowl. Add the milk, cream, grated cheese, chopped bacon, and chopped onion. Mix and season well with salt and pepper.

When the pastry has finished cooking, remove the dishes from the halogen oven and remove the waxed paper and baking beans. Pour the egg mixture evenly into the ramekins, place a slice of tomato on each one, and sprinkle with more salt and pepper. Return the ramekins to the halogen oven on the low rack. Cook at 375°F for 20 minutes, then 5 minutes more at 300°F. Serve immediately or let cool as desired.

NOW TRY THIS...

BROCCOLI AND BLUE CHEESE

Make up the quiche bases and mixture as above, adding 6 broccoli florets and 1/2 cup crumbled blue cheese instead of bacon and cheddar. Cook as directed above.

SMOKED SALMON

Make up the quiche bases and mixture as above, but omit the shredded cheddar cheese, bacon, and onion, and add in 2 1/2 cups cream cheese and 1/2 cup diced smoked salmon instead. Cook as directed above.

BRIE AND CRANBERRY

Make up the quiche bases as above. Place 3 slices of brie around the base of each, spread with 2 tsp. cranberry jelly, then pour over the egg mixture, omitting the cheese, bacon, and onion. Cook as directed above.

Croque Monsieur

The traditional French ham and cheese sandwich is ideal for cooking in the halogen oven. It will be crisp and golden on the outside and succulent on the inside.

6 tbsp. finely shredded Swiss cheese, such as Gruyère

2 tbsp. sour cream or crème fraîche

salt and freshly ground black pepper

1/2 tsp. Worcestershire sauce

1/2 tsp. Dijon mustard

4 slices white sandwich bread, buttered

2 thin slices deli ham

Makes 2 sandwiches

In a small bowl, mix the cheese with enough cream or crème fraîche for it to hold together. Add the seasoning, Worcestershire sauce, and mustard, and mix until combined.

Place 2 slices of bread butter-side down on the oven tray. Divide the cheese mixture between them, and spread it right to the edges. Add the deli ham, cutting it to fit, if necessary. Cover with the other 2 slices of bread, butter-side up, to make 2 sandwiches. Press down lightly. Place the oven tray on the high rack of the halogen

ANOTHER WAY

To make a Croque Madame, add a fried egg to the sandwich just before cooking.

oven and cook at 400°F for 3–4 minutes. Turn the sandwiches over and cook for 3–4 minutes more, or until golden brown on the outside and melting on the inside.

Halloumi Kebabs

These Greek cheese kebabs are great if you have a vegetarian guest coming for dinner. They can be prepared in very little time in advance, then popped into the halogen oven to cook quickly and evenly. These kebabs are delicious with a salad and baked potatoes.

4 wood skewers, soaked in hot water for 10 minutes before use

8 oz. halloumi cheese

1/2 red onion

16 sun-dried tomatoes in oil

1 small can pineapple chunks, drained

Serves 2

Cut the cheese and red onion into cubes. Drain the tomatoes and reserve the oil. Alternate the halloumi, onion, sun-dried tomatoes, and pineapple on the 4 soaked skewers. Place the skewers on the round baking tray and brush all over with 1 tbsp. of the sun-dried tomato oil.

When ready to cook, place the baking tray on the low rack of the halogen oven. Cook for 15 minutes at 450°F, turning every 5 minutes. Remove and serve 2 skewers per person.

TIP

Soaking the skewers before use prevents the food from sticking to them, but more importantly, stops the wood skewers burning under the fierce halogen light.

Spicy Penne with Artichokes

The artichokes and sun-dried tomatoes add a flavor reminiscent of the Mediterranean to this spicy pasta dish. The tomato sauce is so versatile, it can be used with many of the dishes in this book. This is a great dish for vegetarians.

12 oz. dried penne pasta

1/2 cup quartered canned artichokes

1/2 cup halved sun-dried tomatoes

1/4 cup freshly chopped basil, plus more to serve

2 red chiles, seeded and finely chopped, or to taste

freshly grated Parmesan cheese, to serve

Tomato Sauce

2 tbsp. olive oil

1 large onion, finely chopped

2 cloves garlic, crushed

2 (16-oz.) cans chopped tomatoes in sauce

2 (5-oz.) cans tomato paste

2 tsp. soy sauce

2 tsp. Worcestershire sauce

2 tsp. dried mixed Italian herbs

2 tsp. sugar

salt and freshly ground black pepper

2 chicken or vegetable stock cubes

Serves 4

Make the tomato sauce. In a large saucepan, heat the oil. When it is hot but not smoking, add the onion and garlic, and cook over medium heat until the onion has softened, about 10 minutes. Add the tomatoes, cover, and simmer gently for 15 minutes. Add the tomato paste, soy sauce, Worcestershire sauce, Italian herbs, sugar, salt, pepper, and stock cubes. Simmer, covered, for 10 minutes. Remove from the heat and set aside.

Bring a large saucepan of water to a boil, and add the pasta. Cook according to the instructions, until just tender. Drain and tip back into the saucepan. Add the tomato sauce, artichokes, sun-dried tomatoes, basil, and chiles, and stir briefly to combine. Transfer to a casserole dish. Cook, covered with a lid or foil, on the low rack of the halogen oven at 375°F for 30–40 minutes, or until heated through. Serve sprinkled with a little Parmesan cheese and extra chopped basil.

ANOTHER WAY

If you prefer, you can add sautéed sliced chicken breast for extra protein. In a large skillet, heat 2 tbsp. canola oil, and add 1 lb. skinless and boneless chicken breasts, cut into 1/4-inch slices. Add 2 tsp. Cajun seasoning (page 116) and sauté chicken for 10 minutes over medium heat. Add to the pasta just before serving.

Garlic Mushrooms

This is a great low-fat side dish to accompany grilled or broiled steak or chicken. The extra beef stock cube and garlic in the sauce intensify the flavor.

1 lb. mushrooms
2 cloves garlic, crushed
2 shallots, finely chopped
1/4 cup good-quality chicken
   or beef stock
1 beef stock cube
salt and freshly ground black
   pepper
1/4 cup freshly chopped
   parsley, to serve

Remove most of the stalks from the mushrooms, then halve the mushroom caps. Put them in a baking dish and add the garlic, shallots, stock, and stock cube. Cook on the low rack of the halogen oven at 350°F for 20–25 minutes, stirring the mushrooms every 5 minutes while cooking. Season to taste with salt and pepper, and serve immediately, sprinkled with parsley.

ANOTHER WAY

Substitute the chicken or beef stock for 1/4 cup white wine, and use a mix of different varieties of mushrooms.

Serves 4

Ratatouille

This classic French dish works really well in the halogen oven. Roasting the vegetables first on the low rack caramelizes them and helps to bring out the sweetness of the dish.

1 red onion, sliced
1 small eggplant, cubed
1 small zucchini, sliced
2 large tomatoes, cut into wedges
1 yellow pepper, cut into large dice
1 clove garlic, chopped
2 tbsp. tomato paste
1 tbsp. olive oil
pinch mixed dried herbs
salt and freshly ground black
   pepper
3 cups canned chopped tomatoes in
   juice
3 tbsp. tomato ketchup
1 1/4 cups vegetable stock

In a large baking dish that can fit into the halogen oven, mix the red onion, eggplant, zucchini, fresh tomatoes, yellow bell pepper, garlic, tomato paste, olive oil, mixed herbs, and salt and pepper.

   Place the dish in the halogen oven on the lower rack and cook at 440°F for 20 minutes. Stir every 5 minutes as the vegetables begin to roast and caramelize.

   Add the canned chopped tomatoes, ketchup, and vegetable stock. Mix well.

ANOTHER WAY

This dish can be spiced up with some fresh chiles or cayenne pepper. Topped with grated cheese, it also makes a tasty vegetable bake.

Lower the heat to 390°F and cook for 20 minutes, stirring every 5 minutes. Serve hot.

Serves 6

Vegetable Spears with Parmesan Sprinkle

Cut all the vegetables into equal-sized pieces, add plenty of seasoning, and a sprinkling of Parmesan for a delicious accompaniment to roast meat or casseroles.

1 medium carrot
2 medium parsnips
1 medium sweet potato
1 medium potato
1 raw beet
2 tbsp. olive oil
1 tbsp. dried rosemary
salt and freshly ground black
    pepper
2 tbsp. finely grated Parmesan
    cheese

Serves 4

Peel and cut all the vegetables to equal-sized spears, 1/4 inch wide and about 2 inches long. Drop them in the bottom of the glass bowl of the halogen oven, drizzle with olive oil, add the rosemary, and season with plenty of salt and pepper. Bake at 450°F for 30 minutes, or until lightly browned and tender. Stir occasionally. Serve sprinkled with Parmesan cheese.

ANOTHER WAY

For a quick and easy dinner, slice 2 boneless and skinless chicken breasts, season well with salt and freshly ground black pepper, then tuck them among the vegetables as they cook. Check the chicken is cooked through before serving.

Baked Zucchini

This is a very quick side dish to prepare. It is delicious with grilled meats.

2 medium zucchini
1 tbsp. olive oil
salt and freshly ground black
    pepper
1/2 cup shredded Swiss cheese,
    such as Emmental

Serves 4

Top and tail the zucchini and cut into 1/4-inch-thick slices lengthwise. Place on the round oven tray, brush the tops with oil, and sprinkle with salt and pepper. Place in the halogen oven on the low rack and cook at 500°F for 5 minutes per side. Sprinkle with the cheese and cook for a further 3 minutes. Remove from the oven and serve hot.

ANOTHER WAY

For garlic zucchini, add 1 crushed clove of garlic to the oil before brushing the zucchini. For herbed zucchini, sprinkle with dried Italian mixed herbs or oregano. You can also use a different cheese, such as a pepperjack cheese or cheddar.

Squash and Sweet Potato Bake

This can be served as a side dish or as a vegetarian main dish.

1 red onion, sliced
1 small butternut squash, peeled,
    seeded, and cut in small cubes
1 sweet potato, peeled and cubed
2 cloves garlic, finely chopped
1/4 tbsp. celery salt
1 tsp. dried thyme
2 tbsp. olive oil
salt and freshly ground black pepper
1 tsp. cornstarch
2 tbsp. water
1 1/2 cups heavy cream
1/2 cup shredded cheddar cheese

Serves 4

Place the red onion, butternut squash, sweet potato, garlic, celery salt, thyme, olive oil, salt, and pepper in a large bowl. Mix well, then place in a baking dish. Set the baking dish on the lower rack in the halogen oven and cook at 500°F for 20 minutes, stirring every 5 minutes.

Mix the cornstarch with the water, then add the cream and stir. Pour this mixture on top of the roasted vegetables and cook at 500°F for 5 minutes.

Sprinkle with cheese and cook at 350°F for 15 minutes more. Serve hot.

ANOTHER WAY

To make this dish into a more substantial main course, add 1 cup mushrooms, and serve with steamed vegetables. Add 1/4 cup crumbled blue cheese with the cream for a stronger cheese flavor.

Green Bean Casserole

This dish is often made with condensed mushroom soup, but it is so much healthier to make your own sauce. If you cannot find mushroom ketchup, substitute 1 tsp. Worcestershire sauce and an additional 1 tsp. soy sauce.

1 tsp. vegetable oil, for greasing
1 lb. 4 oz. thin green beans (such as
    haricots vert)
1/4 cup butter
1 small onion, finely chopped
1 clove garlic, crushed
1 1/2 cups finely sliced mushrooms
1/4 cup flour
1 3/4 cups milk
2 tbsp. mushroom ketchup
1 tsp. soy sauce
1 chicken stock cube
salt and freshly ground black pepper
1 tbsp. canola oil
1 large onion, finely sliced
1 tbsp. brown sugar
Parmesan cheese, to serve

Serves 6

With a little vegetable oil, grease a casserole dish that will fit inside the halogen oven.

In a large saucepan filled with boiling water, blanch the green beans for 5 minutes, drain, and refresh with cold water. Set aside.

Melt the butter in the saucepan, add the onion and garlic, and cook over a gentle heat for 10 minutes until softened. Add the mushrooms and cook for 5 minutes. Stir in the flour and cook for 3 minutes, stirring continuously. Gradually stir in the milk, incorporating it into the roux and vegetables slowly, then cook over a gentle heat until the sauce has thickened. Add the mushroom ketchup, soy sauce, and chicken stock cube, stirring continuously. Taste the sauce, and season with a little salt and plenty of pepper. Put the drained beans into the casserole dish, pour in the mushroom sauce, and place on the low rack in the halogen oven. Cook for 20–25 minutes at 350°F, or until heated through, stirring every 5 minutes to turn the beans around so that they heat up faster.

Meanwhile, in a large skillet, melt the canola oil, and when it is hot but not smoking, add the sliced onion and cook over a gentle heat for 15 minutes. Add the brown sugar and continue to cook for about 10 minutes. Turn the heat up to high and cook for 2 minutes, stirring continuously, until the onions have browned and are caramelized. Remove from the heat and keep warm.

When the beans are heated through, remove the casserole from the oven, tip the caramelized onions on top, and serve immediately, sprinkled with a little freshly grated Parmesan cheese.

ANOTHER WAY

Make the mushroom sauce into a cheese sauce by omitting the mushrooms and mushroom ketchup, and substituting 1 cup finely shredded cheddar cheese and 1 tsp. Dijon mustard. Also add 1 skinned, seeded, and chopped tomato and 1/2 cup cooked chopped spinach to the beans in the casserole dish before pouring in the sauce.

Focaccia

This is a very wet dough, so it is best when kneaded in a mixer with a dough hook. Any time you need to handle the dough, use oil instead of flour on your hands to prevent it from sticking. This bread needs to be started well in advance. The rye flour is used to add a bit of extra flavor, but regular flour can be substituted.

1/2 tbsp. fresh yeast or 1 tsp. dried yeast
1 cup warm water
1 tsp. sugar
2 cups bread flour
1 tbsp. rye flour
1/2 tsp. salt
3 tbsp. olive oil
1 tsp. dried mixed Italian herbs

Makes 1 round loaf

Mix half the yeast with 3/4 cup water and 1/2 tsp. sugar. Leave for 6 minutes.

Mix in 1 cup flour and the salt, and knead for 5 minutes with the dough hook. Grease the dough ball with 1 tbsp. olive oil, then place in a mixing bowl and cover with plastic wrap. Leave for 12 hours or overnight in a warm place.

After 12 hours, mix the remaining yeast with the remaining 1/4 cup water and 1/2 tsp. sugar. Leave for 6 minutes. Mix in remaining flour and knead for 5 minutes. Combine this dough with the first dough and knead for 5 minutes. Rub with 1 tbsp. olive oil, place in the mixing bowl, cover with plastic wrap, and let rest in a warm place for 2 hours.

Place on a greased round baking tray, cover with 1 tbsp. olive oil, and make indentations with your thumb about 20 times. Sprinkle the indentations with the dried herbs. Leave in a warm place to rise for 20 minutes.

Preheat the halogen oven to 500°F for 3 minutes. Lower the heat to 350°F, place the baking tray on the low rack, and cook for 25 minutes. Turn the bread over, raise the heat to 425°F, and continue to cook for 7 minutes. Remove and let cool until ready to serve.

ANOTHER WAY

This is delicious with the creamy spinach casserole (page 111), or just enjoyed on its own, dipped in a little olive oil.

DINNER

Mediterranean Roast Chicken

Lemon, rosemary, and garlic are classic Mediterranean flavors. Cooking chicken with lemon brings out all its flavors and helps tenderize it.

1 (3–4 lb.) chicken, washed
    and patted dry
1 lemon, halved
1 tbsp. olive oil
1 tbsp. chopped fresh
    rosemary
1/2 tsp. garlic salt
salt and freshly ground black
    pepper

Serves 4

Squeeze the lemon over the chicken, then rub the chicken skin with the olive oil, chopped rosemary, and garlic salt, and salt and pepper to taste. Stuff the chicken with the remaining lemon. Place the chicken directly on the low rack in the halogen oven. Cook at 440°F for 45 minutes, turning it over every 15 minutes, then turn it down to 360°F for the rest of the cooking time (about another 45 minutes) or until thoroughly cooked.

Rest in the halogen oven, turned off, for 10 minutes, before carving and serving.

NOW TRY THIS...

BACON-WRAPPED ROAST CHICKEN

Follow the recipe above, omitting the lemon. Before cooking, cover the chicken with strips of streaky bacon. The bacon will help baste the chicken and keep the flesh succulent. Cook as directed above, making sure to check that the chicken is cooked through and the juices run clear.

ROAST CHICKEN WITH LEMON, GARLIC, AND TARRAGON

Follow the recipe as above, adding 1 tbsp. chopped fresh tarragon to the garlic salt. Rub the mixture over the chicken, season with salt and freshly ground black pepper, and cook as directed above.

SAFFRON AND LEMON CHICKEN

Mix together 1 tsp. ground coriander, 1/2 tsp. garlic salt, 1/4 tsp. ground ginger, 1/4 tsp. saffron threads, and 2 tbsp. olive oil. Follow the recipe as above, rubbing the saffron mixture over the chicken after squeezing over the lemon. Cook as directed above.

GARLIC BUTTER ROAST CHICKEN

Make 1/2 cup garlic butter (page 112). Soften, then spread over the chicken. Sprinkle with 1 tbsp. chopped fresh rosemary, and season with salt and freshly ground black pepper. Cook as directed above.

Stuffed Chicken Wrapped in Pancetta

A rich walnut and mushroom stuffing transforms chicken breasts into a wonderfully filling dish, ideal for a sophisticated dinner party or an everyday dinner.

4 chicken breasts
1 tbsp. olive oil
1 cup finely chopped mushrooms
1 shallot, finely chopped
1 clove garlic, crushed
1/4 cup chopped walnuts
3 tbsp. freshly chopped parsley
salt and freshly ground black
   pepper
8 slices pancetta
olive oil to drizzle

Red Wine Sauce
1 tbsp. olive oil
2 shallots, finely chopped
1 1/4 cups red wine
1/4 cup port wine
1/2 cup good-quality chicken
   stock
2 tbsp. red currant jelly
1 tbsp. tomato paste
2 tsp. cornstarch mixed with
   2 tbsp. water

Serves 4

With a sharp knife, cut a slit in the side of each chicken breast to make a pocket. Set aside.

In a medium skillet, heat the oil over a low heat, then sauté the mushrooms, shallots, and garlic until soft. Remove from the heat, add the walnuts, parsley, and salt and pepper. Let cool. Stuff the mixture into the chicken pockets, then wrap 2 slices of pancetta around each chicken breast to hold them together. Place the chicken breasts on a greased ovenproof dish and drizzle with a little olive oil and season with a little more salt and pepper. Place on the low rack of the halogen oven and turn the temperature to 400°F. Switch the timer to 35 minutes. Turn the chicken over halfway through cooking time.

While the chicken is cooking, make the red wine sauce. In a medium saucepan, heat the oil and fry the shallots for 5 minutes until softened. Add the red wine, port wine, and stock, and simmer until the liquid has reduced by two-thirds. Add the red currant jelly and tomato paste and stir until dissolved. Add the cornstarch mixed with a little water and bring back to a boil, stirring until thickened.

Serve the chicken with the red wine sauce.

NOW TRY THIS...

CHICKEN CORDON BLEU

Open out the chicken breasts. Place 1 slice deli ham and 1 slice low-fat cheddar cheese on each breast. Fold the chicken breasts over in half, so that the ham and cheese is enclosed inside. Dredge each breast in flour, before dipping it in beaten egg and covering in breadcrumbs. Place on a plate, cover, and chill for at least an hour, or until required. Place the chicken on a greased oven tray, and cook at 375°F on the low rack of the halogen oven for 20 minutes. Turn the chicken over, and cook for another 20 minutes, or until golden brown. Serve immediately.

Bourbon and Maple Chicken

The intense heat from the halogen lamp lends an amazing flavor to this dish, caramelizing the sugar in the sauce and making it irresistible.

1 chicken, cut into 8 pieces,
    and skinned
1/3 cup red wine
4 tbsp. soy sauce
2 tbsp. red wine vinegar
1 tbsp. tomato paste
2 tbsp. maple syrup
2 tbsp. bourbon
1 tsp. ground ginger
1 tsp. dry mustard
2 cloves garlic, crushed
watercress, to serve

Serves 4

Place the chicken on the round oven tray and cook on the high rack of the halogen oven at 425°F for 15 minutes, turning the chicken over halfway through cooking time.

In a medium bowl, whisk together the red wine, soy sauce, vinegar, tomato paste, maple syrup, bourbon, ginger, mustard, and garlic, until well combined. Spoon half the sauce over the chicken and cook for 5 minutes at 425°F. Then lower the heat to 375°F and cook for another 5 minutes, then turn the chicken over and spoon on the remaining sauce. Cook 5 minutes more, then transfer the chicken to a serving plate and keep warm in a low oven. Pour the sauce from the oven tray into a small saucepan, place over medium heat, and bring to a boil. Simmer for 5–8 minutes, until the sauce has reduced in volume. Serve the chicken immediately, with the sauce poured on top, and garnished with watercress. This dish goes well with basmati rice with added chopped red bell pepper and a small finely chopped onion, and garnished with freshly chopped green onions.

ANOTHER WAY

If you would rather not use alcohol in this dish, substitute good-quality chicken stock for the red wine and omit the bourbon.

Coconut Chicken with Sweet Chile Dip

The coconut in this dish creates a wonderful, fragrant aroma—it is so exotic no one will guess it was cooked in a halogen oven!

8 skinless and boneless chicken
   thighs
1 tbsp. lime juice
2 tsp. garam masala
1/4 cup flour
salt and freshly ground black
   pepper
1/2 cup breadcrumbs
1/2 cup flaked coconut
1 egg, lightly beaten

sweet chili sauce, to serve

Serves 4

Trim any visible fat from the chicken thighs and check there are no small bits of bone left. Cut each thigh in half. Place on a plate, sprinkle with the lime juice and garam masala, and let marinate while you continue the preparation. Place the flour on a plate and season with salt and pepper. On another plate, mix the breadcrumbs and coconut. Put the egg on a third plate. Pat the chicken dry with paper towels, and roll each piece in the seasoned flour. Place in the beaten egg and then in the breadcrumb and coconut mix.

Find a heatproof sheet pan that will fit inside your halogen oven and spray it lightly with cooking oil. Place the breaded chicken on the sheet, and spray

ANOTHER WAY

For an easy variation on this dish, omit the lime juice and chili sauce and use 1 tbsp. Cajun seasoning (page 116), in the breadcrumbs.

lightly with the oil. Place the pan on the high rack, turn on the heat to 400°F, and switch the timer to 35 minutes. After about 15 minutes, turn the chicken over with tongs. Cook for the remaining 15–20 minutes, or until browned and crispy. Serve with the chili sauce.

Lemon Chicken

This is a wonderful Chinese dish to cook quickly on a busy weeknight.

2 chicken breasts, cubed
1 tbsp. soy sauce
2 tbsp. plum sauce
1 tbsp. lemon juice

For the Sauce
1/4 tbsp cornstarch
2 tbsp. cold water
2 tbsp. rice vinegar
2 tbsp. plum sauce
1/2 tbsp. sugar
1 cup good-quality chicken stock
4 tbsp. lemon juice
1/2 lemon

In a large mixing bowl, combine the cubed chicken with the soy sauce, plum sauce, and lemon juice. Tip mixture onto the round oven tray and cook on the low rack in the halogen oven at 500°F for 12 minutes. Stir, then cook for 3 minutes more.

Meanwhile, mix the cornstarch with the cold water, then add the rice vinegar, plum sauce, sugar, chicken stock, and lemon juice. Grate the zest from the half lemon into the mixture, then

ANOTHER WAY

This lemon sauce also makes an excellent accompaniment for white fish fillets.

slice the lemon and add to the sauce mixture. Mix the sauce and pour it over the chicken. Cook for a further 8 minutes at 400°F. Serve immediately with steamed rice.

Moroccan-Spiced Butterfly Quail

Quails are very small birds, so you need to serve one per person. You could substitute tiny chickens if you cannot find quails.

2 cloves garlic, crushed
1 tbsp. ground cumin
1 tbsp. ground coriander
1 tbsp. ground cinnamon
1 tbsp. paprika
salt and freshly ground black
    pepper
2 tbsp. olive oil
4 quails, spatchcocked

Serves 4

Wash and pat dry the quails. In a small bowl, mix the garlic and spices together. Wipe olive oil and then pat on garlic and spice mixture all over each quail.

Place the birds on the oven tray, and cook on the low rack at 400°F for 10 minutes each side, or until the birds are cooked through. Depending upon the size of the birds, you may need to do this in batches, so keep them warm while you cook the rest of the birds. Serve immediately.

TIP

To butterfly or spatchcock a chicken or another bird, first turn the bird upside down and cut along one side of the backbone with kitchen shears or a sharp knife. Rotate the bird around, and cut along the other side of the backbone, then cut it away. Open the bird up like a book, and find the diamond-shaped breastbone. Cut along both sides of the breastbone, run your fingers along either side, and pull it out. You might need to cut it away from the breast meat underneath. Trim away any excess fat from either side of the bird, and it is ready to cook.

Duck Breasts with Red Currant Sauce

The sweetness of the red currant sauce complements the stronger flavor of the duck breast. Serve with steamed vegetables and mashed potatoes.

1 onion, finely chopped
1 tsp. olive oil
2 duck breasts
a pinch of salt
1/2 tbsp. cornstarch
2 tbsp. cold water
1 chicken stock cube
1 1/4 cups boiling water
3 tbsp. red currant jelly
1/2 tbsp. brown sugar

Serves 2

Mix the chopped onion with the olive oil and place on the round baking tray. Score the skin of the duck breasts and rub with salt. Place ducks on top of the onion and cook at 450°F in the halogen oven on the low rack for 15 minutes. Turn the duck breasts over and cook for 5 minutes more.

Mix the cornstarch in the cold water. Dissolve the stock cube in the boiling water. Mix the dissolved cornstarch, stock, red currant jelly, and brown sugar to a smooth liquid.

Turn the duck breasts back over, cover with the sauce, and cook for an additional 5 minutes. Turn off the oven and allow the duck to rest for 5 minutes, still in the oven. Remove and serve with the sauce.

ANOTHER WAY

The halogen oven is perfect for cooking meat in this way. Try using this method and sauce with lamb chops or steaks.

Lemon and Oregano Pork Escalopes

Pork coated in breadcrumbs and baked in the halogen oven stays moist inside and crunchy on the outside, and is delicious served with lemon or garlic mayonnaise.

1 1/4 lbs. pork fillet, in 1 or 2 pieces
1/4 cup flour
salt and freshly ground black pepper
2 eggs, beaten
finely grated zest of 1 lemon
2–3 cups fresh breadcrumbs
2 tsp. dried oregano
1 tsp. sunflower oil, for greasing
spray oil

Serves 4

Cut the pork into 8 slices, about 1 inch thick, and place them between sheets of parchment paper. Beat with a kitchen mallet or a rolling pin until they are about 1/4 inch thick. Set out 3 plates. On the first, put the flour, seasoned with salt and pepper; on the second, put the beaten egg; and on the third, mix together the lemon zest, breadcrumbs, and oregano. Dip each pork escalope first in the flour, then into the egg, and finally roll in the breadcrumbs, until well coated.

Lightly grease the oven tray with sunflower oil, and add 4 escalopes at a time. Cook at 400°F on the high rack of the halogen oven for 5 minutes,

TIP

To make garlic or lemon mayonnaise, just add 1 minced clove of garlic or 1 tsp. lemon zest to 5 tbsp. mayonnaise.

turn the escalopes over, spray with a little oil, and cook for another 5 minutes, or until the breadcrumbs are browned and crisp and the pork is cooked through. Keep warm while you cook all the escalopes. Serve with either garlic or lemon mayonnaise.

Slow Roasted Belly of Pork

This cut of meat needs lots of time and little attention. It is best when cooked slowly, for at least 5 hours. The skin should crisp to form cracklings and the fat should melt away.

2 lbs. 4 oz. belly of pork
4 sprigs fresh rosemary
2 sprigs fresh thyme
1 tsp. chopped dried bay leaves
3 cloves garlic, halved
freshly ground black pepper
1 tbsp. salt, for rubbing the meat

Serves 4

Ask the butcher to score the skin, if it has not been done already. If you have to do it yourself, use a very sharp craft knife or box cutter.

Place the pork, skin-side down, on the oven tray. Distribute the rosemary, thyme, bay leaves, and garlic evenly over the meat of the belly. Season with plenty of pepper. Press a sheet of aluminum foil over the belly flesh to make sure the garlic and herbs will not move. Turn the whole lot over, so the skin side is up, and form the foil into a snug cocoon around the pork, leaving the skin exposed and ensuring that the meat is completely enclosed. Rub the surface with the salt.

ANOTHER WAY

If you like cracklings, after cooking turn the heat back up to 450°F and cook for 5 minutes more.

Cook on the low rack of the halogen oven for 5 minutes at 450°F. Turn the heat down to 250°F, leave the pork on the low rack, and cook for a further 5 hours. Let the pork rest for 15 minutes before serving.

Greek-Style Roast Lamb

This wonderful, hearty dish of lamb, tomatoes, and olives is full of Mediterranean flavors. It is best served with rice and salad.

1 red onion, sliced

1 tbsp. oil

1 (2-lb.) leg of lamb

2 sprigs fresh rosemary

5 cloves garlic, sliced

salt and freshly ground black pepper

2 cups canned chopped tomatoes

2 tbsp. chopped olives (use your favorite variety)

1 tsp. dried oregano

2 tbsp. white wine vinegar

1 tsp. sugar

3 tbsp. water

Serves 4

Place the sliced onion on a greased round baking tray. Make narrow cuts into the lamb on all sides. Stud the lamb with the rosemary and garlic, season with salt and pepper, and place it on top of the onions. Cook on the low rack of the halogen oven at 460°F for 15 minutes. Turn the lamb over and cook for an additional 15 minutes.

Mix the tomatoes, olives, dried oregano, vinegar, sugar, and water together.

Lift up the lamb and place this tomato mixture underneath. Lower the oven temperature to 350°F and cook the lamb on the low rack for a further 40 minutes for rare lamb. Cook for an additional 40 minutes for well-done lamb.

Turn off the oven and allow lamb to rest in the oven for a further 10 minutes, then serve with the sauce.

ANOTHER WAY

If you like a sweeter sauce for the lamb, add 1 tbsp. honey with the tomatoes.

Lamb Brochettes with Basil and Oregano

Lean lamb, rolled in basil and oregano, is threaded onto skewers with red bell pepper and broiled until slightly charred on the edges but still slightly pink in the center.

1 lb. 4 oz. lean lamb, from
   the leg
1 tbsp. dried basil
1 tbsp. dried oregano
1 large red bell pepper, seeded
   and cut into 1-inch pieces
2 tbsp. olive oil
salt and freshly ground black
   pepper
Béarnaise sauce, to serve

Serves 4

If using wooden skewers, soak for 10 minutes in cold water. Cut the lamb into 1-inch cubes. On a plate, mix together the basil and oregano. Roll the lamb cubes in the herbs. Thread the lamb, alternating with the bell pepper pieces, onto 6–8 skewers. Do not pack them too close together; leave a bit of a gap. Place on a plate and drizzle with the olive oil. Leave covered in the refrigerator to marinate for at least 30 minutes, or longer if you have time. Transfer the skewers to the oven tray, season with a little salt and plenty of pepper, and broil at 400°F on the high rack of the halogen oven for 4–5 minutes. Turn over and broil for another 4–5 minutes, or until slightly

ANOTHER WAY

Newly picked herbs add a delightful freshness to the taste of any dish. Try fresh thyme and rosemary instead of dried basil and oregano, and red onion in place of red bell pepper. Vary the vegetables according to season, preference, and availability.

chargrilled on the edges but still a little pink in the center. Serve immediately, with your favorite Béarnaise sauce.

Lamb Steaks with Herb Crust

The crunchiness of the breadcrumb coating works well with the texture of the lamb. These steaks are great with mashed potatoes and a tossed salad.

4 lamb steaks (1 inch thick)
2 tbsp. honey
1 tsp. Dijon mustard
1/2 cup fresh white
   breadcrumbs
2 tsp. freshly chopped parsley
salt and freshly ground black
   pepper
1 tbsp. olive oil, plus a little for
   greasing pan

Serves 4

Place the lamb steaks on the round baking tray and cook on the high rack in the halogen oven at 500°F for 4 minutes per side. Remove steaks and let them drain on paper towels.

Mix together the honey and mustard in a bowl. In a separate bowl, combine the breadcrumbs, parsley, salt, pepper, and 1 tbsp. olive oil. Wipe the remaining oil on the clean round oven tray.

Brush the honey mustard on both sides of each lamb steak, then dredge each steak in the crumb mixture until evenly coated. Place the steaks on

ANOTHER WAY

Add 1/2 tsp. dried oregano to the breadcrumb coating or try other types of mustard, such as wholegrain or yellow mustard.

the greased oven tray and cook on the low rack of the halogen oven at 350°F for 3–5 minutes per side, or until they are done to your preference. Serve immediately.

Rack of Lamb with Rosemary and Garlic

Rosemary and garlic are perfect partners for this succulent roast lamb, cooked to perfection.

1 (2-lb.) rack of lamb
2 sprigs fresh rosemary
1 whole garlic bulb (top cut off)
olive oil

Red Currant Sauce
1 tbsp.olive oil
2 shallots, finely diced
14 oz. red currants
1/2 cup red wine
1/2 cup chicken stock

Serves 4

Place the lamb on the low rack in the halogen oven and cover with the rosemary. Place the garlic on its stalk next to the leg, drizzle everything with olive oil, and cook at 460°F for 10 minutes. Turn the lamb over, reduce the temperature to 350°F, and cook for 20 minutes. Turn again and cook for a further 20 minutes for pink, 25 minutes for medium, or 30–35 minutes for well-done. Remove the lamb from the oven and let rest in a warm place for a few minutes before serving.

To make the sauce, fry the shallots in a small skillet with a little olive oil until translucent, then add the red currants. Cook until they burst, then add the red wine and chicken stock. Increase the heat and reduce the sauce by about half, then strain into a small serving dish.

Serve the lamb with the warm red currant sauce, with peas and mashed potatoes.

TIP

With any kind of roast meat, resting is essential. Think of the resting time as part of the cooking time and plan accordingly. It can actually be helpful to have a few minutes to assemble the other components of the meal.

Filet Mignon with a Trio of Sauces

Steak can be served with a choice of sauces or plain if you prefer. We have chosen three of our favorite sauces—pepper sauce, blue cheese sauce, and herb butter.

1 filet mignon
1 tbsp. oil
salt and freshly ground black
    pepper

Pepper Sauce
1/4 tsp. crushed or coarsely
    ground black peppercorns
1/2 cup heavy cream
2 tbsp. steak sauce
a pinch of salt

Blue Cheese Sauce
2 tbsp. blue cheese, crumbled
1/2 cup heavy cream
pinch freshly ground black
    pepper

Herb Butter
2 tbsp. butter, softened
2 tbsp. freshly chopped parsley

Serves 1

Brush the steak with the oil and season to taste with salt and pepper. Place on the round baking tray, set it on the high rack of the halogen oven, and cook at 500°F for 5 minutes on each side (or to your taste). While the steak is cooking, prepare the sauce you're using.

Pepper Sauce

Mix together all the ingredients, and pour over the cooked steak. Cook for a further 5 minutes at 500°F.

Blue Cheese Sauce

Break the blue cheese into pieces, then mix with the cream, season with pepper, pour over cooked steak, and cook for a further 5 minutes at 500°F.

Herb Butter

Mix the butter and parsley together. Check the steak is done and place a dollop of the butter on top when ready to serve.

ANOTHER WAY

To make a delicious Cajun seasoning for steak, mix together
1/2 tsp. ground sea salt
1 tbsp. paprika
1 tbsp. cayenne pepper
1/2 tsp. garlic salt
1/2 tbsp. freshly ground black
    pepper
1/2 tbsp. ground white pepper
1/2 tsp. ground mustard
1/4 tsp. pumpkin pie spice
1 tsp. dried basil
Place the steak in a large bowl with 1 small red onion, sliced, 1/2 tbsp canola oil, and 1 tbsp Cajun seasoning. Mix well. Allow to marinate for at least 10 minutes or overnight. Place the marinated steak with the onions on a round oven tray, cook on the high rack at 480°F for:
• Rare: 5 minutes on each side
• Medium: 7 minutes each side
• Well done: 10 minutes on each side.

Rib Roast with Red Wine Gravy

A rib roast works so well in the halogen oven. The radiant heat seals the outside and makes it succulent and juicy on the inside. No need to pan-fry first!

1 (2-lb.) rib roast (2 ribs)
1 tbsp. butter
salt and finely ground black
    pepper
4 cloves garlic, sliced
1/2 cup red wine
1–2 beef stock cubes mixed
    with 1 1/2 cups boiling
    water
1 tsp. sugar
1 tsp. dried Italian mixed herbs
1 onion, finely chopped
1 tbsp. cornstarch

Serves 4

Rub the beef with the butter and sprinkle with salt and pepper. Pierce the beef all over and stud with the pieces of sliced garlic.

Pour the red wine and beef stock into the base / glass bowl of the halogen oven. Stir in the sugar, mixed herbs, and onions.

Place the beef directly on the low rack in the halogen oven and cook at 460°F for 20 minutes, turning every 10 minutes. Then lower the heat to 350°F and cook for an additional 30 minutes, turning every 10 minutes. If you want rare meat, remove the roast from the oven. For medium doneness, continue cooking the beef for 20 minutes more, or 35 minutes for well-done meat.

Let the beef rest. Remove the low rack from the halogen oven. Mix a little water with the cornstarch, then stir into the red wine mixture in the base of the halogen oven. Cook for 5 minutes at 500°F to make a gravy. Add the beef to the gravy, turn off the heat, close the lid of the halogen oven, and let the meat rest, in the oven, for 10 minutes, before serving.

ANOTHER WAY

If you don't want to use wine, replace it with 1/2 cup beef stock.

Thai Fish Cakes

These spicy and flavorful little fish cakes are wonderful as a starter or as a main course. Serve with sweet chili sauce for dipping.

1 tsp. canola oil, for greasing
1 lb. 2 oz. white fish fillet(s)
1 egg, lightly beaten
2 tbsp. cornstarch
1 tbsp. fish sauce
1–2 tsp. red Thai curry paste, or
   to taste
1 tsp. seeded and finely chopped
   red chile
2 tbsp. freshly chopped cilantro
salt and freshly ground black
   pepper
2 green onions, chopped
sweet chili sauce, to serve

Makes 8–9

Lightly brush the oven tray with canola oil. Chop the fish into 1/2-inch pieces, and place into a food processor. Pulse until coarsely chopped. Add egg, cornstarch, fish sauce, curry paste, chile, and cilantro, and season with salt and pepper. Pulse a few times until combined. Mix in the onions. Using your hands, form into small fish cakes about 3 inches in diameter. Place them on the oiled oven tray, set it on the high rack of the halogen oven, and cook at 440°F for 5 minutes per side, or until lightly browned, and cooked through. Keep warm while you cook all the fish cakes. Serve with sweet chili sauce.

TIP

Make your own red Thai curry paste by processing 2 shallots, 2 cloves garlic, 2 red chiles, 1-inch piece fresh gingerroot, 1 tbsp. fish or soy sauce, 1 tsp. each ground coriander and cumin, 1 chopped lemongrass stalk, zest and juice of 1 lime, and salt and freshly ground black pepper. Cover and store any surplus in the refrigerator for up to 1 week, or freeze for up to 1 month.

Tilapia with Parmesan Crust

In the halogen oven this topping becomes a lovely crispy crust that helps to keep the fish really succulent while complementing the flavor of the fish.

4 tbsp. fresh breadcrumbs
2 tbsp. freshly grated Parmesan
   cheese
1/2 tbsp. chopped fresh oregano
1/2 tbsp. chopped fresh parsley
2 tbsp. olive oil, plus a little more
   for greasing
1 tbsp. freshly squeezed lime juice
2 (8-oz.) tilapia fillets

Serves 2

Mix the breadcrumbs, Parmesan, oregano, and parsley together in a bowl. Stir in the oil and lime juice to make a paste.

Lightly rub a round baking dish with the remaining oil. Place the tilapia fillets in the dish. Spread the paste on top of the fillets, covering them evenly. Place the dish in the halogen oven on the low rack and cook at 440°F for 12 minutes, or until the fillets are thoroughly cooked.

Serve immediately, with a green salad.

ANOTHER WAY

This is an easy dish to vary. You can use other white fish fillets such as cod, or sea bass. Also, try other herbs, such as thyme, dill weed, or chives.

Haddock and Cheese Ramekins

This dish is even better when half the haddock is smoked. A considerable amount of haddock is smoked, especially in Scotland, but you may not be able to find it in other parts of the world.

vegetable oil, for greasing
12 oz. fresh haddock fillet (or
  6 oz. fresh and 6 oz.
  smoked, if possible)
1 cup water
4 tbsp. dry white wine
1 fish stock cube
6 peppercorns
1 bay leaf
1 shallot, finely sliced
1/4 cup butter
2 cups finely sliced mushrooms
2 tbsp. flour
freshly ground black pepper
1/2 cup finely shredded
  cheddar cheese
1/2 cup fresh breadcrumbs

Serves 4

Grease 6 ramekins (4 inches in diameter) with a little vegetable oil.

In a large saucepan, place the fish with the water and wine. Add the fish stock cube, peppercorns, bay leaf, and shallot, and bring to a boil. Cover and poach gently for about 12 minutes.

Strain off the liquid and reserve. Flake the fish, discarding the skin and any bones. Discard also the peppercorns, bay leaf, and shallot. In a medium saucepan over medium heat, melt the butter, add the mushrooms, and sauté for 5 minutes. Stir in the flour and cook gently for 2 minutes, stirring continuously. Lower the heat slightly, and gradually add the strained cooking liquid. Bring to a boil and continue to cook, stirring, until the sauce thickens. If it thickens too much, add a little water or white wine. Add half the cheese, and season to taste with salt and pepper, stirring until the cheese has melted. Gently fold in the fish, spoon the mixture into the prepared ramekins, and top with the remaining cheese and crumbs. Place 3 on the oven tray on the low rack of the halogen oven at 350°F. Cook for about 8 minutes, or until golden brown and nice and hot. Keep warm while you cook the other 3. Serve immediately.

ANOTHER WAY

This dish can be made with any available firm-fleshed white fish. You could also try using a mixture of salmon and shrimp, and adding a little freshly chopped parsley to the sauce.

Pesto-Crusted Cod

The intense heat of the halogen oven helps to cook the fish very quickly while keeping it from becoming dry and tough. You can use any white fish in place of the cod fillets.

2 cod fillets

Pesto
2 cloves garlic
2 tbsp. grated Parmesan cheese
2 tbsp. pine nuts
salt and freshly ground black
    pepper
2 large handfuls fresh basil
    leaves
4 tbsp. olive oil, plus a little
    extra for greasing

Serves 2

To make the pesto, chop the garlic with the Parmesan in a food processor. Add the pine nuts and the salt and pepper to taste, and process. Add the basil leaves and oil, and process to your desired consistency.

Lightly grease a round baking dish. Place the cod fillets in the dish and spread the pesto on top of the fish. Place in the halogen oven on the low rack and cook at 440°F for 12 minutes or until the fillets are thoroughly cooked. Serve with a green salad.

TIP

The pesto will keep up to 3 days in a sealed container. It is also great with cooked penne pasta.

Grilled Sole and Lemon

Fish cooks so well in the halogen oven. The quick heating up of the oven cooks it quickly, but seals in the juices, keeping the fish from drying out. This recipe is good with boiled new potatoes and steamed sugarsnap peas or another green vegetable.

2 medium-sized sole fillets
    (or flounder)
1 tbsp. butter, softened
salt and freshly ground black
    pepper
1 lemon, cut into 6 wedges
1 tbsp. freshly chopped parsley

Serves 2

Rub sole fillets with butter and season with salt and pepper. Place them on the round baking tray. Arrange the lemon wedges around the fillets.

Place the tray on the low rack of the halogen oven and cook at 400°F for 15 minutes, turning over halfway through. Serve the fillets with the grilled lemon and sprinkled with chopped parsley.

ANOTHER WAY

Five minutes before the end of cooking, brush a spoonful of red or green pesto over the fish.

Butter-Roasted Monkfish

Monkfish is a firm, meaty white fish that is simply delicious when roasted in a hot halogen oven. This will be a family favorite in no time at all.

2 cups monkfish, cubed

1 tbsp. sweet chili sauce

1/4 tsp. mixed dried Italian herbs

a pinch of salt and pepper

1 tbsp. melted butter

juice of 1 lime

1 large onion, cut into 1-inch squares

1 red bell pepper, cut into 1-inch squares

12 cherry tomatoes

4 cups fresh spinach leaves

Serves 4

Place the cubed monkfish in a bowl and add sweet chili sauce, mixed dried herbs, salt and pepper, butter, and half the lime juice. Mix and leave to marinate for 10 minutes, then place on the round oven tray with the onion, red bell pepper, and cherry tomatoes. Place on the high rack at 440°F for 8 minutes. Take out and place in a bowl.

Place the spinach on the round oven tray and place the monkfish, peppers, onion, and cherry tomatoes on top. Cook for a further 4 minutes at 440°F or until cooked. Use the rest of the juice of the lime on the monkish and serve on a bed of salad.

NOW TRY THIS...

TUNA AND SESAME SEED SALAD

Follow the recipe above, substituting 2 cups diced tuna fish steak for the monkfish. Cook as directed. Sprinkle the tuna fish with toasted sesame seeds before serving on a bed of salad.

SEAFOOD MEDLEY

Cook as directed above, substituting 1 cup mixed scallops and shrimp for half the monkfish.

SPICY MONKFISH

Follow the recipe above, adding 1/2 tsp. ground cumin and 1/2 tsp. dried red chile flakes along with the mixed herbs. Cook as directed above.

MOROCCAN MONKFISH

Follow the recipe above, adding 1/2 tsp. ground cumin along with the mixed herbs. Cook as directed above. Serve with couscous.

Salmon and Bell Pepper Sauté with Tomatoes

Fish, bacon, and bell peppers with tomatoes and cheese make an interesting combination for dinner, sure to be enjoyed by children and adults alike.

1 tbsp. canola oil, plus extra
   for greasing
1 1/2 lbs. oily fish fillets, such
   as salmon
1/4 cup flour
salt and freshly ground black
   pepper
4 strips bacon, chopped
1/2 green bell pepper, sliced
3 tomatoes, skinned and
   quartered
1/2 cup shredded cheddar
   cheese

Serves 4

Grease a baking dish that will fit in your halogen oven with a little canola oil.

Cut the salmon fillet into pieces, each about 2 inches. Season the flour with salt and pepper. Toss the salmon in the seasoned flour.

Cook the bacon and bell pepper together in the halogen oven on the oven tray on the high rack at 420°F for 5 minutes, stirring halfway through. Transfer to the baking dish. Add the fish to the oven tray and drizzle with a little canola oil. Cook in the halogen oven for 3 minutes on each side, taking care not to break it up. Transfer the fish to the baking dish, add the tomatoes, and season to taste with salt and pepper. Sprinkle the cheese on top, and return the baking dish to the oven to cook on the high rack at 350°F for a further 5 minutes, or until heated through completely. Serve immediately.

ANOTHER WAY

Replace the salmon with any firm-fleshed white fish. An excellent choice would be a combination of salmon, cod, and shrimp.

Roasted Mediterranean Vegetables

The halogen oven is perfect for roasting these vegetables, as they char beautifully on the edges, hold their shape well, and remain succulent and full of flavor.

1 small eggplant, cubed
1 zucchini, quartered lengthwise
    and sliced
1 red bell pepper, seeded and cut
    into 1/2-inch pieces
1 small red onion, peeled and cut
    into wedges
1 tbsp. olive oil
salt and freshly ground black pepper
6–8 cherry tomatoes
2 tbsp. freshly chopped basil leaves

Serves 4

Lightly grease the oven tray, and add the eggplant, zucchini, pepper, and onion pieces. Drizzle with the olive oil, season with salt and pepper, and place on the low rack of the halogen oven. Cook for 10 minutes at 400°F. Turn the vegetables over, add the tomatoes, and cook for 5–10 minutes more, or until the vegetables are lightly charred on the edges and tender. Just before serving, sprinkle with freshly chopped basil.

TIP

If you have two dishes to cook, and only one oven, you can prepare this dish up to the last 5 minutes. It will heat up quickly, while you are serving another dish.

Eggplant Parmigiana

This wonderful Italian dish is a good example of how you can create a meal in one dish with the halogen oven, whereas the conventional way would use many pans.

1 medium eggplant, sliced
4 tbsp. olive oil
1/2 onion, chopped
1 clove garlic, chopped
4 cups canned chopped tomatoes
    in juice
4 tbsp. tomato ketchup
1 tsp. mixed dried Italian herbs
salt and freshly ground black
    pepper
1/2 cup freshly grated Parmesan
    cheese
1 handful fresh oregano (optional)

Serves 4

Place the eggplant slices on the round oven tray, brush with a little oil, and cook on the low rack in the halogen oven at 500°F for 6 minutes on each side. Remove and set aside.

In an ovenproof baking dish, cook the onion with 1 tbsp. olive oil for 3 minutes at 500°F on the low rack. Add the garlic and 1/2 tbsp. olive oil, cook for 1 minute, then add the chopped tomatoes, ketchup, mixed herbs, and season to taste. Cook for 5 minutes. Remove from the oven, stir, and pour half the sauce into a bowl.

Layer eggplant slices on top of the sauce remaining in the baking dish. Cover with some

ANOTHER WAY

Add 1/4 cup chopped chorizo to the tomato sauce for extra depth of flavor and spice.

Parmesan and some of the tomato sauce, then repeat this process. Finish with the remaining Parmesan and cook on the low rack at 350°F for 20 minutes. Remove from the oven, cut into slices, and serve immediately with a sprinkling of fresh oregano.

Potato Dauphinoise with Swiss Cheese

This is a rich, creamy, and tasty dish, well suited to special occasions. It is included here to show that you can cook potato casseroles in the halogen oven, although it is necessary to parboil the potatoes first.

2 lbs. potatoes, such as Russets

2 tbsp. butter, softened, plus extra for greasing

1 medium onion, finely chopped

3 cups finely shredded Gruyère cheese

salt and freshly ground black pepper

2/3 cup plus 2 tbsp. half-and-half

Serves 4–5

Grease a shallow baking dish that will fit inside your halogen oven.

Peel the potatoes, leave them whole, and parboil them for 10 minutes in a large saucepan filled with boiling water. Drain and let cool for 10 minutes. Slice the potatoes as thinly as possible without letting them fall apart. Put a layer of potato slices, overlapping, in the bottom of the dish. Dot with butter, sprinkle with some of the onion and cheese, and season with salt and pepper. Pour in about a quarter of the half-and-half. Continue with these layers until all the ingredients have been used up, finishing with a layer of cheese and pouring the remaining half-and-half over the top.

Cover with a lid or buttered foil, and bake on the low rack of the halogen oven at 400°F for 50 minutes, or until the potatoes are tender when pierced with a skewer. Remove the lid or foil cover, turn the heat up to 425°F, and cook until the top layer of cheese is bubbling. Watch carefully, as this may only take 2 or 3 minutes.

ANOTHER WAY

For a less expensive, less rich dish, substitute cheddar cheese and milk for the Gruyère and cream. You could also add garlic and parsley to the layers if you wish.

Roasted Potatoes with Rosemary

Potatoes roasted in the halogen oven are crispy on the outside and light and fluffy on the inside. Why not try different variations by adding spices, herbs, and oils?

6 large potatoes, peeled and
    quartered
1/2 cup melted duck fat, lard,
    or shortening
1/2 tsp. sea salt
pinch white pepper
1 sprig fresh rosemary

Serves 4

In a medium saucepan half-filled with boiling water, cook the potatoes for 10 minutes. Drain, replace the potatoes in the pan, pour in the melted fat or shortening, and season with salt and pepper. Cover the pan and shake to roughen the edges of the potatoes.

Place the potatoes on the round oven tray on the low rack of the halogen oven and cook at 500°F for 20 minutes. Turn over the potatoes, sprinkle with the fresh rosemary needles, and cook for an additional 25 minutes. Remove and serve immediately.

ANOTHER WAY

This is good with sweet potatoes too, either alone or mixed with the white potatoes. Sweet potatoes will take less time to cook: cook for 15 minutes at 500°F, then turn, and cook for a further 20 minutes.

Honey Parsnips

The halogen oven really helps to caramelize the honey and sweeten up the parsnips. These are great served with roast meats.

4 parsnips, peeled and
    quartered
2 tbsp. olive oil
salt and freshly ground
    black pepper
3 tbsp. honey

Serves 4

Place parsnips, olive oil, salt, and pepper in a large bowl and mix together. Tip onto the round oven baking tray. Place on the lower rack in the halogen oven at 500°F and cook, stirring every 5 minutes, for 15 minutes.

Drizzle with the honey, stir, and cook for an additional 10 minutes. Serve hot.

ANOTHER WAY

To add a little something extra, garnish before serving with toasted sesame seeds.

Grilled Asparagus Wrapped in Parma Ham

Asparagus spears are so tasty wrapped with the Parma ham, this makes a great dipping food.

16 asparagus spears
16 slices Parma ham
a pinch of salt and pepper
1 tbsp. canola oil
1/2 tbsp. fresh parsley, chopped

Dipping Sauce
2 tbsp. sweet chili sauce
4 tbsp. cream cheese
2 tbsp. mayonnaise

Serves 4

Put the asparagus in a suitably sized bowl and pour boiling water over the spears. Leave for 5 minutes.

Remove the asparagus from the water and wrap each spear in a slice of Parma ham. Place on a round oven tray, season, and drizzle with oil. Grill the wrapped asparagus on high rack at 460°F for 4 minutes.

ANOTHER WAY

This dip also makes the perfect accompaniment for tortilla chips.

For the dipping sauce, mix the sweet chili sauce, cream cheese, and mayonnaise together and serve.

Creamy Spinach Casserole

The creaminess of the cheese goes beautifully with the wilted spinach, making this a quick and easy dish to prepare and a great way to get kids to eat spinach.

4 cups (8 oz.) baby spinach
2 tbsp. olive oil
1/4 tsp. garlic salt
1 1/2 cups cream cheese
3 tbsp. milk
1/2 tsp. dried mixed Italian
    herbs

Serves 4

Combine the spinach, oil, and garlic salt in a baking dish. Cook in the halogen oven on the low rack at 500°F for 3 minutes.

Mix the cream cheese and milk together. Stir into the spinach along with the Italian herbs and cook for 5 minutes more, still at 500°F. Serve hot.

ANOTHER WAY

Add some crispy bacon sprinkles for added flavor. This also makes a great appetizer with crusty bread.

Quick Dinner Rolls

Nothing can be nicer than smelling freshly baked bread, especially when you have guests. This easy recipe is ideal for dinner parties, but it's so easy you can make it for a simple family dinner.

2 tsp. fresh yeast or 1 tsp. dried yeast

2/3 cup warm milk (110°F)

1 tsp. sugar

2 cups all-purpose or bread flour, plus extra for kneading

1/2 tsp. salt

1/4 cup melted butter or oil, plus more for greasing

Optional Flavorings

1 tsp. chopped garlic

2 tsp. chopped olives (Kalamata preferred)

3 tsp. chopped sun-dried tomatoes

Makes 8

Mix the yeast with the milk and sugar. Leave for 6 minutes to dissolve.

Place the flour and salt in a large mixing bowl and mix in the melted butter. Add the yeast liquid and mix to a soft dough. Knead the dough on a lightly floured counter for 7 minutes, or until it becomes firm and elastic. To save time, you can use a freestanding mixer with a dough hook.

Let the dough rise in the mixing bowl, covered with a clean damp cloth. Leave in a warm place for 10 minutes, so the dough will expand. Knead the dough again for 2 minutes to reduce it to its original size. Now you can add your chosen flavoring to the dough, kneading to combine thoroughly. Shape into small rolls and place on a greased round oven tray.

Cook rolls in the halogen oven on the low rack at 440°F for 15–25 minutes or until thoroughly cooked. The cooking time will vary depending on what size rolls you make. Let cool before serving.

ANOTHER WAY

Flavored butter goes perfectly with these rolls. To make garlic butter, take 1/2 cup unsalted butter, and melt slightly. Finely chop 3 cloves garlic and mix into the butter. You can also add other chopped herbs—try 1 tsp. dried oregano or 2 tsp. chopped fresh parsley. Place the garlic butter on a sheet of baking parchment, roll into a cylinder, and refrigerate until ready to use.

SNACKS & DESSERTS

Potato Skins with Bacon and Cheese

A filling dish that makes a great snack or appetizer.

4 medium baking potatoes
4 strips bacon
1 small onion, finely chopped
2 tbsp. mayonnaise
2 tsp. cream cheese
salt and freshly ground black
    pepper
2 oz. cheddar cheese, shredded

Serves 4

Wash and dry the potatoes, and place them on the low rack in the halogen oven. Cook at 500°F for 45–60 minutes, turning every 15 minutes or until thoroughly cooked. Remove and slice in half lengthwise. Set aside to cool slightly.

Place the bacon on the round oven tray and cook on the low rack at 450°F for 4 minutes per side. When cooked and crisp, chop the bacon.

With a small spoon, scoop out some of the cooked potato, leaving the skins intact. Mix the potato in a bowl with the chopped bacon, onion, mayonnaise, cream cheese, and salt and pepper to taste. Fill the potato skins with the mixture. Sprinkle with the shredded cheddar cheese.

When ready to serve, cook the potatoes on the high rack at 500°F for 5 minutes or until hot and golden brown.

TIP

These can be made in advance but will need 10 minutes' more cooking time and will need to be cooked on the low rack of the halogen oven.

Crispy Potato Fries

Potato fries cooked in the halogen oven are so good—crispy on the outside and fluffy on the inside. The addition of Cajun seasoning adds depth to the flavor and a touch of spiciness.

Cajun Seasoning
1/2 tsp. white pepper
1/2 tsp. garlic powder
1/2 tsp. onion powder
1/2 tsp. ground red pepper
1/2 tsp. paprika
1/2 tsp. black pepper

4 medium potatoes, peeled, sliced, and cut into thick strips
1 tbsp. canola oil
salt and freshly ground black pepper

Serves 4

Make the Cajun seasoning by combining the ingredients in a small bowl.

In a large bowl, place the potatoes, add the oil, and sprinkle on the Cajun seasoning. Add a little salt and plenty of freshly ground black pepper, and stir with a wooden spoon to coat the potatoes completely. Transfer to the round oven tray and bake, stirring occasionally, on the low rack of the halogen oven at 500°F for 25 minutes, or until browned and crispy.

ANOTHER WAY

Vary the seasonings on the fries, using black mustard seeds or crushed cardamom seeds instead of Cajun spice. Or sprinkle with fresh herbs at the end of cooking time. You could even sprinkle with a little finely shredded cheddar cheese.

Spicy Potato Wedges with Sour Cream Dip

Nothing can be nicer than sitting down watching a movie with these wedges and a sour cream dip. These are also delicious with ketchup, ranch dressing, or garlic mayonnaise.

2 medium potatoes, cut into wedges
1 tbsp. mayonnaise
1 tbsp. sweet chili sauce
3 tbsp. olive oil
1 tbsp. cayenne pepper, or to taste
pinch garlic salt
salt and freshly ground black pepper
1/2 cup sour cream
2 tbsp. minced fresh chives

Serves 2

Place the potato wedges in a large mixing bowl. Combine the mayonnaise, sweet chili sauce, and olive oil with the seasonings, then mix well with the potatoes. Place the seasoned wedges on the round oven tray, and set the tray on the low rack in the halogen oven. Cook at 500°F for 25 minutes, stirring occasionally, or until tender and golden brown.

While the potatoes are cooking, mix the sour cream with the chives. Keep chilled in a small

TIP

You can peel and cut the potatoes in advance, but they must be kept in water to prevent browning.

serving bowl until ready to serve. Serve the wedges immediately while hot with the sour cream dip.

Nachos with Salsa

A treat for when you sit around with friends watching a movie. You can substitute any favorite cheese, such as Monterey Jack or pepperjack, if you want. This is good with sour cream and chive dip (page 116) or guacamole (page 44).

Salsa

2 ripe tomatoes, chopped and
    seeded
2 green onions, sliced
2 tbsp. olive oil
1 tbsp. lime juice
1 sliced jalapeño pepper
1 tbsp. freshly chopped cilantro
salt and freshly ground black
    pepper

Nachos

1 bag favorite tortilla chips
1 cup shredded cheddar cheese

Serves 4

In a medium bowl, combine the salsa ingredients, check the seasoning, and add more salt and pepper as needed. Let stand a while to meld the flavors together.

Pour the bag of chips into an ovenproof dish, spoon the salsa over the top, then sprinkle with the shredded cheese. Cook in the halogen oven on the low rack at 400°F for 8 minutes. Remove and serve immediately.

NOW TRY THIS...

VEGETABLE FEAST NACHOS

In a skillet, fry 1 small zucchini, diced, and 1/2 small red bell pepper, sliced. Add to the salsa ingredients listed above, along with 1 small can sweetcorn. Cook as directed above.

SPICY NACHOS

Follow the recipe as above, adding 1 tsp. hot sauce, such as Tabasco, to the salsa. Spoon the salsa over the chips, then sprinkle over 1/2 cup diced chorizo, before adding the cheese. Cook as above.

MUSHROOM NACHOS WITH REFRIED BEANS

Place 1 cup sliced portobello mushrooms in a small skillet, with 1 tsp. olive oil, 1 tbsp. soy sauce, and 1 tsp. lemon juice. Fry gently until the mushrooms are soft. Drain. Follow the recipe as directed above, but spoon 1 cup refried beans over the chips before adding the salsa. Next add the cooked mushrooms and the shredded cheese. Cook as above.

GREEK NACHOS

Follow the recipe, adding 1/4 cup sliced black or green olives to the salsa, and omitting the lime juice and jalapeño pepper. Substitute 1/2 cup crumbled feta cheese for the shredded cheese. Cook as directed above.

Tomato Bruschetta

Chopped tomatoes with a touch of garlic and a little chopped basil spooned onto crispy garlic bread make a fresh and healthy accompaniment to a breakfast or brunch buffet. This is a great way to use up day-old French bread.

1 1/2 cups chopped Roma tomatoes
3 tbsp. finely chopped red onion
1 large clove garlic, minced or finely
    chopped
2 tbsp. freshly chopped basil
4 tbsp. extra-virgin olive oil
1/2 tsp. red wine vinegar
salt and freshly ground black
    pepper
1 tsp. garlic salt
1/2 French baguette loaf, cut
    diagonally into 6 1/2-inch slices

Makes 6 slices

In a large bowl, mix together the tomatoes, onion, garlic, basil, 2 tsp. olive oil, and the red wine vinegar. Season with a little salt and pepper, cover, and chill in the refrigerator for about 2 hours.

In a small bowl, mix the remaining olive oil with the garlic salt and brush it over both sides of each slice of bread. Toast the bread on the high rack of the halogen oven at 425°F for 1–2 minutes per side, until nicely browned. Remove from the oven and allow to cool. Arrange the slices on plates, and spoon the tomato mixture carefully onto each slice. Serve immediately.

ANOTHER WAY

If you prefer a more substantial bruschetta, cut the bread into 3/4-inch slices. Replace the basil with cilantro, and add a little finely chopped chile for a spicy alternative. You could also add diced bell pepper or chopped olives to the mixture.

Bacon-Wrapped Mushrooms

These ever-popular party hors d'oeuvres are quickly made in a halogen oven.

16 mushrooms
1 large mozzarella ball, cut into
    16 pieces
16 strips bacon
1 tbsp. olive oil

Makes 16

Clean the mushrooms and remove the stalks. Fill the center of each mushroom with a piece of mozzarella. Wrap each mushroom with a strip of bacon and secure with a toothpick. Rub the mushrooms with a little olive oil.

To cook, place directly on the low rack of the halogen oven for 14 minutes at 400°F, turning them over after the first 7 minutes of cooking. Serve immediately.

ANOTHER WAY

Use chicken liver pâté instead of mozzarella to stuff the mushrooms.

Popcorn

Low-fat, high-fiber, and so much fun to make in your halogen oven, this is one recipe you'll use time and time again.

1/2 cup popping corn

Serves 4

Preheat the round tray to 480°F and cook the popping corn on the tray on the low shelf of the halogen oven for 8 minutes. Leave to rest in the halogen oven for 5 minutes to ensure all of the corn has popped (a few may not pop). Remove and pour into a serving bowl. Serve plain, or with one of the toppings listed below.

NOW TRY THIS...

SWEET MAPLE SAUCE

In the base of a small heatproof bowl place 1/4 cup brown sugar, 2 tbsp. maple syrup and 1 tbsp. butter. Place this on the round oven tray on the low rack in the halogen oven. Cook the sauce at 480°F for 3 1/2 minutes. Remove and set aside. Use an oven mitt to hold the bowl still, and whisk the sauce with a fork for a full 2 minutes until the ingredients are fully mixed to form the maple sauce. Pour over popcorn while still warm, or use as a dipping sauce.

SIMON AND GARFUNKEL

Pound together 1 tsp. each dried parsley, sage, rosemary, and thyme. Sprinkle herb powder over the hot popcorn.

HOTCORN

Mix together 2 tsp. cayenne pepper, 2 tsp. paprika, and 1 tsp. garlic powder. Sprinkle over hot popcorn.

POPCORN–MARSHMALLOW BAR

After popping your corn, mix 1 cup marshmallows with 1 tbsp. butter and melt in a heatproof bowl in the halogen oven. Combine marshmallow–butter mixture with popcorn, press into a greased baking pan and let cool for 10 minutes. Cut into 12 bars.

POPPY ROAD

Melt 3 oz. milk chocolate over a pan of simmering water on the stove, and mix with 2 tbsp. candied cherries, 2 tbsp. golden raisins, and 2 tbsp. chopped pecans. Mix the popcorn in. Drop spoonfuls of the mixture onto a cookie sheet and let cool.

COLORED CORN

If you want to make colored popcorn, melt a small knob of butter on the round tray. Add 2–3 drops food coloring to the butter, then add the popping corn kernels.

Chocolate Brownies

These cakelike brownies are crunchy on the outside, because they are cooked on both sides, while being soft and chewy in the middle.

3/4 cup butter

7 oz. bittersweet chocolate

3 eggs

1/2 cup dark brown sugar

1/4 cup chocolate powder
    (such as Nesquick)

2 tbsp. coffee liqueur

1/2 cup flour

Serves 6

Line an 8-inch round oven tray and an 8-inch steamer tray (or a second oven tray) with baking parchment paper. Using a little of the butter, grease both pieces of parchment paper.

Add a cup of boiling water to the base of the halogen oven. Place the bittersweet chocolate in a heatproof bowl. Place the remaining butter on top. Place the bowl on the low rack and cook at 400°F for 5 minutes. Stir to combine the chocolate and butter, cook for 2 minutes more, then remove the bowl and stir again. Leave the boiling water in the base of the halogen oven.

Whisk the eggs and sugar together in a large bowl. Add the chocolate powder, melted chocolate mixture, and coffee liqueur. Stir to combine, then fold in the flour. Pour the brownie mixture into the prepared round tray. Place the tray on the low rack and bake at 320°F for 20 minutes. Remove, then, place the lined steamer tray over the top of the part-cooked brownie and turn over, keeping the brownie sandwiched between the two round trays. Put it back into the halogen oven and cook for a further 15 minutes at 350°F to cook the base, which is now facing up. Once cooked, remove from oven, turn back over, slice, and serve hot with cream or ice cream.

ANOTHER WAY

To make extra-indulgent chocolate-frosted brownies, mix together:

2 cups confectioners' sugar

1/2 cup unsalted butter at
    room temperature

2 tbsp. cocoa powder

1/2 tsp. vanilla extract

1 tbsp. whole milk

Spread the frosting on top of the brownies, and leave to set before serving.

Lavender Shortbread Cookies

Shortbread-style sugar cookies are a popular treat with children, and ideal for making in the halogen oven. The subtle flavor of lavender gives a fashionable twist to an old favorite.

1 cup (2 sticks) unsalted butter, softened, plus extra for greasing
1 cup sugar
1/2 cup confectioners' sugar
1 large egg, lightly beaten
1 tbsp. freeze-dried dehydrated lavender flowers, crushed to a powder
2 1/2 cups flour
1 tsp. baking soda
1 tsp. cream of tartar
pinch nutmeg

Makes about 50

In a large bowl, with an electric mixer, cream the butter and sugars together until light and fluffy. Beat in the egg and the crushed lavender. Sift together the flour, baking soda, and cream of tartar, and stir into the creamed mixture. Chill for 2–3 hours or overnight.

Grease the oven tray with a little butter. Roll out about a quarter of the cookie dough on a floured surface to 1/4-inch thickness, and cut out with a 2-inch cookie cutter. Place on the oven tray and cook in the halogen oven on the high rack at 300°F for 10 minutes. Turn off the oven and leave the cookies in the oven for 3 minutes. Then remove the tray from the oven and let the cookies cool on the tray for 3 minutes, before transferring them to a wire rack to cool completely. Wash and dry the oven tray. Repeat until you have used up all the dough. Cool on a wire rack and store in an airtight container.

ANOTHER WAY

If you cannot find lavender flowers, or lavender-flavored sugar, use both 1 tsp. vanilla extract and 1 tsp. almond extract instead. Divide the dough and keep the rest covered and chilled in the refrigerator. Roll out only a quarter of the dough at a time, and work quickly, as the dough will get sticky as it warms up.

Cherry Kuchen

This is a quickly prepared, moist cherry cake, rich with butter and vanilla flavors, and delicious served with coffee, warm or cold, on its own, or as part of a brunch buffet.

1/2 cup (1 stick) unsalted
   butter, softened
1/2 cup sugar
1 large egg
1 cup flour
1/2 tsp. baking powder
1 tsp. vanilla extract
a little milk, if needed
1/2 of 1 (16-oz.) can dark
   cherry pie filling
2 tbsp. sliced almonds
confectioners' sugar, to serve

Serves 6

In a large bowl, beat the first six ingredients together to make a fairly thick batter. If the batter seems too thick, thin it with a little milk. Pour most of the batter into the bottom of a greased 8-inch baking pan. Pour the cherry pie filling on top, and drop the remaining batter on top of the cherries. Scatter the sliced almonds on top. Bake on the low rack at 300°F for 20 minutes, turn the heat up to 325°F and cook for 20 minutes, or until golden brown, and cooked through. Cool in the pan for 5 minutes before cutting into 6 slices. Dust with confectioners' sugar to serve.

NOW TRY THIS...

APRICOT AND ALMOND KUCHEN

Prepare the basic recipe, adding 1 tsp. almond extract to the batter. Instead of the cherry filling, drain 1 can apricots. Heat juice with 2 tbsp. cornstarch and 2 tbsp. orange juice until boiling and thickened. Chop apricots, add to the juice, and cool before using.

PLUM KUCHEN

Prepare the basic recipe, omitting the cherries. Substitute 1 lb pitted and chopped plums, stewed gently in a little water and a little sugar to taste. Cool before using.

APPLE AND CINNAMON KUCHEN

Prepare the basic recipe, replacing the butter with 8 fl oz vegetable oil. Instead of the cherry filling, stew 2 peeled and sliced apples with 2 tbsp. sugar and 2 tsp. cinnamon. Cool before using.

RHUBARB KUCHEN

Prepare the basic recipe, omitting the cherries. Substitute 1 lb sliced rhubarb, stewed in a little orange juice and sugar to taste. Cool before using.

Apricot and Ginger Upside Down Cake

This wonderfully sticky cake is great with afternoon coffee, or with cream for a delicious dessert.

Sponge Mix
3/4 cup all-purpose flour
2 tsp. baking powder
1/2 cup (1 stick) butter
2 eggs
1/2 cup superfine sugar

Base
3 tbsp. maple syrup
1 tbsp. butter
1/3 cup crystallized stem ginger
5 candied cherries
1 (14-oz.) can apricot halves,
    drained
butter, for greasing

Serves 5

Mix sponge ingredients in a food mixer or in a large bowl with a wooden spoon until creamed together. Divide the maple syrup, butter, candied cherries, stem ginger, and apricots between 5 ramekins greased with butter. Place the cake mix on top.

Place 1/2 inch water in the base of the halogen oven. Place the ramekins in the halogen oven on the lower rack. Cook at 325°F for 45–55 minutes or until a skewer inserted comes out clean. Turn out when cooked, upside down, on a plate.

NOW TRY THIS...

PINEAPPLE UPSIDE DOWN CAKE

Prepare the basic recipe, omitting the ginger and replacing the glacé cherries and apricot halves with 1 (14-oz) can pineapple chunks.

PLUM UPSIDE DOWN CAKE

Prepare the basic recipe, substituting 12 oz plums, stewed in a little water, with 3 tbsp. maple syrup for the apricot base.

APRICOT AND ALMOND UPSIDE DOWN CAKE

Prepare the basic recipe, omitting the ginger. When cooked, turn out the cakes and sprinkle with toasted flaked almonds.

SPICED PEAR UPSIDE DOWN CAKE

Peel, core, and quarter 6 ripe pears. Place in a medium sized pan with 16 fl oz red wine, 2 tbsp. soft brown sugar, 1 cinnamon stick, and 1 vanilla pod. Simmer gently for 30–40 minutes, or until the pears are tender. Drain the juice and use the pears in place of the apricot mix. The pear juice can be reduced, sweetened, and used as a sauce.

Marsala and Amaretto Peaches

Peaches are quite often a little difficult to catch right at that moment when they are ripe, soft, and succulent. So when they are a little hard, bake them in sweet marsala wine, and serve very cold with chilled mascarpone and fromage frais, mixed with honey.

4 firm but ripe peaches
1 cup sweet marsala wine
2 tbsp. amaretto liqueur
4 tbsp. sugar
2 tbsp. honey
1 tsp. cornstarch
2 tsp. water
4 tbsp. Italian mascarpone, room temperature
4 tbsp. fromage frais or Greek yogurt
3 tbsp. honey

Serves 4

Halve the peaches, remove the pits, and place the peaches in a large bowl. Cover with boiling water, leave for 1 minute, drain, and slide the skins off. Place them in a shallow baking dish. In a medium bowl, mix the marsala with the amaretto, sugar, and honey, and pour it over the peaches. Bake, uncovered, on the low rack at 325°F for 25–30 minutes. Remove from the halogen oven and set aside to cool for 10 minutes.

Place the peaches on a serving dish, cover, and place in the refrigerator. Pour the wine and sugar syrup into a small saucepan. Bring to a boil. In a small bowl, mix the cornstarch with the water, and add it to the syrup, stirring, until it thickens. Set aside to cool, then pour it over the peaches. Chill until really cold, about 6 hours.

In a medium bowl, mix the mascarpone, fromage frais, and honey, until well combined. Cover and chill until required.

Serve 2 peach halves per person, with the sauce spooned over, and mascarpone mix on the side.

ANOTHER WAY

For a nice variation, replace the peaches with unpeeled nectarines. Add 1 tbsp. mascarpone and 2 tsp. light brown sugar to each nectarine half, pour 1/3 cup peach schnapps around the nectarines, and bake as per the recipe.

Chocolate Rum Bananas

These are easy to prepare in advance for a dinner party. Your guests will love the taste of the melted chocolate with the gooey banana.

2 tbsp. dark brown sugar
2 tbsp. rum
4 bananas
12 milk chocolate squares
4 scoops vanilla ice cream

Serves 4

Cut 4 (12-inch) squares of tin foil. Mix the sugar and rum together. Peel the bananas and place each one on a square of tin foil. Cut along the length of each banana to form a pocket. Fill the pocket with 3 chocolate squares and sprinkle with the sugared rum. Close the tin foil to form a tight pouch and cook on the low rack in the halogen oven at 500°F for 10 minutes.

Carefully remove the bananas from their pouches and place them on serving plates. Serve hot with a scoop of ice cream.

ANOTHER WAY

To make this for kids, replace the rum with hot chocolate. To make a healthier variation you could also use raisins or golden raisins instead of chocolate squares.

Baked Apples

This is such a nice warming dessert in winter with cream poured over the top. In the summer, serve the apples with ice cream.

4 cooking apples
1/2 cup raisins
1 tbsp. brown sugar
1/2 tsp. ground cinnamon
2 tbsp. maple syrup
1 tbsp. butter

Serves 4

Core the apples and peel a little around the top, making a bigger hole. Set them on the round oven tray. In a small bowl, mix the raisins, brown sugar, and cinnamon. Stuff the apples with the mixture. Drizzle all over with the maple syrup, then place a bit of butter on each apple.

Place the tray on the low rack of the halogen oven and cook at 325°F for 35 minutes. Remove and serve hot.

ANOTHER WAY

Add 1/4 cup chopped pecans or walnuts or chopped dried apricots and only 1/4 cup raisins to the filling for a change.

Chocolate Bread Pudding with Irish Cream Sauce

The title of this dessert just does not do it justice. This is a chocolate, praline, and cream, succulent and gooey extravaganza, a sweet to inspire poets.

Irish Cream Sauce
1 cup whipping cream
4 tbsp. Irish cream liqueur
2 tbsp. sugar
1 tsp. vanilla extract
1 tsp. cornstarch
2 tsp. water

Bread Puddings
butter for greasing
3 large eggs
1/3 cup sugar, plus more for
    sprinkling
2 tsp. vanilla extract
1 1/2 cups whipping cream
1/3 cup whole milk
8 cups 3/4-inch cubes of
    French bread
4 oz. bittersweet chocolate,
    finely chopped
4 oz. praline-filled milk
    chocolate, chopped (such as
    Guylian)

Serves 6

Make the sauce. In a medium saucepan over a medium heat, bring the cream, liqueur, sugar, and vanilla to a boil. In a small bowl, mix the cornstarch and water to a paste, and whisk into the cream mixture. Simmer gently for 3 minutes until thickened, stirring continuously. Remove from the heat, cool, and transfer to a small bowl. Chill in the refrigerator for at least 2 hours.

Grease 6 ramekins (3–4 inches in diameter) with a little butter.

Make the bread puddings. In a large bowl, whisk together the eggs, sugar, vanilla, 1 cup cream, and milk. Add the bread and chocolates and stir to combine. Let stand for 30 minutes, stirring occasionally. Divide mixture equally between the ramekins, and drizzle with the remaining 1/2 cup cream. Sprinkle each one with a little sugar, and bake on the low rack at 350°F for 20 minutes, or until slightly golden, and the custard is set. If the top looks like it is darkening too much, turn the heat down to 300°F for the last 5–10 minutes. Let stand for 10 minutes, then serve the dessert warm, with the chilled sauce.

ANOTHER WAY

Substitute white chocolate for the praline-filled milk chocolate and challah for the French bread. Add 1/2 cup dried cherries to the mixture before soaking.

Lemon Delight

This very lemony dessert separates as it cooks into a sponge with a lemon sauce underneath.

6 tbsp. unsalted butter, plus
    extra for greasing
1/2 cup sugar
zest and juice from 1 1/2
    lemons
1 rounded tbsp. flour
2 eggs, separated
just under 2/3 cup milk
confectioners' sugar, to serve

Serves 4

Grease 4 ramekins (3–4 inches in diameter) with a little butter. Place a shallow baking pan on the low rack of the halogen oven and pour in enough water to cover the base.

In a medium bowl, cream the remaining butter and sugar with the lemon zest until pale and creamy. Add the flour and lemon juice, and mix well. In a separate bowl, whisk the egg yolks with the milk, then whisk the mixture slowly, a little at a time, into the butter–sugar mixture. Whisk the egg whites with an electric beater until firm, not stiff, and fold into the batter.

Divide the mixture between the ramekins and place on the baking pan. Bake at 350°F for 10 minutes, then turn the heat down to 325°F and cook for 15 minutes, or until the top has turned a golden brown and the bottom has set. Sprinkle with confectioners' sugar and serve immediately.

ANOTHER WAY

Serve with fresh raspberries and whipped cream for a stunning dessert. For a change, use orange juice and orange zest instead of lemon. For a sophisticated dinner party dessert, replace 1 tbsp. of the milk with orange liqueur.

Cherry and Chocolate Cobbler

Chocolate desserts are always a winner, especially with children. This one, like most, is delicious served with vanilla ice cream.

1/2 cup (1 stick) butter, softened, plus a little more for greasing
1/2 cup sugar
1 large egg
1 cup flour
1 tbsp. unsweetened cocoa powder
1 tsp. baking powder
a pinch of salt
1 tsp. vanilla extract
1 (16-oz.) can cherry pie filling
a little milk, if needed
confectioners' sugar and vanilla ice cream, to serve

Serves 8

Grease 8 ramekins (3-4 inches in diameter) with a little butter.

In a medium bowl, whisk together the butter, sugar, egg, flour, cocoa powder, baking powder, salt, and vanilla to make a thick batter. If it seems too stiff, thin it with a little milk.

Divide 2/3 of the batter between the ramekins, then spoon on the cherry pie filling, dividing it equally between the dishes. Spoon on the rest of the batter.

Cook 4 ramekins at a time, on the low rack of the halogen oven, at 315°F for about 20 minutes, or until the cobbler has set. Remove from the oven, and keep warm while you cook the remaining ramekins. Sprinkle with confectioners' sugar, and serve warm with vanilla ice cream.

ANOTHER WAY

For a healthier option, substitute canola oil for the butter.

To vary the flavors you can substitute other fruit pie fillings for the cherry, or use a fruit compote made by lightly cooking together a selection of fruits and berries with a little sugar until they are soft and blended together.

INDEX